She Who Dwells Within

She Who Dwells Within

A FEMINIST VISION
OF A
RENEWED JUDAISM

Lynn Gottlieb

HarperSanFrancisco
A Division of HarperCollinsPublishers

FIRST EDITION

Illustrations by Rebekah Dewald

Library of Congress Cataloging-in-Publication Data
Gottlieb, Lynn.
She who dwells within : a feminist vision of a renewed Judaism / Lynn Gottlieb.
p.   cm.
Includes index.
ISBN 0–06–063292–5 (pbk.: alk. paper)
1. Feminism—Religious aspects—Judaism.   2. Women in Judaism.
3. Judaism—United States.   I. Title.
BM729.w6G68   1995   94–36296
296'.082–dc20   CIP

94 95 96 97 98 ❖ RRD(H) 10 9 8 7 6 5 4 3 2 1
This edition is printed on acid-free paper that meets the American National Standards Institute Z39.48 Standard.

To my mother, Tzivia, of blessed memory
Who opened the door to the wonder of stories

And to my beloved son, Nataniel Tzvi,
Whose presence in my life
Fills me with constant joy

And to Jewish women, past and present,
Who struggled to preserve their culture
As well as their right to live in a just world.

Contents

Acknowledgments

THIS BOOK IS the result of a twenty-year rabbinic and storytelling practice in relationship to thousands of people and a host of communities throughout the United States, Canada, Europe, and Israel. Each time a community or organization offered me the opportunity to share my vision of Judaism I was affirmed along the way. I would especially like to thank Temple Beth Or of the Deaf for the chance to serve as a pulpit rabbi, beginning in the fall of 1973, along with the Hebrew Association of the Deaf and the folks at Mishkan-A Shul, which I established to serve unaffiliated Jewish artists on the Lower East Side of Manhattan.

Thank you to Irene Fine for introducing me to my editor at Harper-Collins and to Ellen Umansky for writing the foreword and for their steadfast friendship and support throughout the years. I would also like to thank Harvey Marks, Sheila Weinberg, Hannah and Daniel Siegel, Levi Kelman, Debbie Miles, Mira Rafalovicz, Flor Fernandez, Sharon Niederman, Diana Davidson, Mathew Sneddon, and Sam and Jo Ellen Howarth, the folks in the New York Havurah. Thanks also to the circles of storytellers with whom I have shared the swapping ground, to my congregation, Nahalat Shalom, for their ongoing love and support, to my teachers and especially to Everett and Mary Gendler, Zalman Shachter-Shalomi, Michael Klein-Katz, Wolf Kelman, may his memory be a blessing, and finally, to all my students young and old who have provided the challenge and inspiration to try to create a feminist vision of a renewed Judaism, I would like to express my heartfelt gratitude.

I would also like to thank my editor Kandace Hawkinson who tended to this project from its inception and without whom this book would not have come to pass. Thanks also to Rebecca Dewald who lent her friendship and artistic vision to *She Who Dwells Within,* and to editorial assistant Andrea Lewis, production editor Mimi Kusch, and copyeditor Holly Elliot who all contributed to the production of this book.

And of course, to my son, Nataniel, who patiently endured my time away and who still refers to God by the pronoun *She.*

Foreword

by Ellen M. Umansky

FOR THOSE OF US who remember the early years of Jewish feminism in the United States, it seems hard to believe that it has been almost twenty years since the nationally organized Jewish Feminist Organization (JFO) came into existence. Seeking "nothing else than the full, direct, and equal participation of women at all levels of Jewish life," the short-lived JFO served as a catalyst for the full-blown emergence of Jewish feminism in this country. Although Jewish feminism ceased to exist as a national movement with the dissolution of the JFO in 1976, as a perspective it continues to grow and has become a significant voice for change. The goals of the Jewish Feminist Organization have not yet been realized completely. Certainly, however, American Jewish women have achieved more than many of us thought possible twenty years ago.

In 1972—the year that Lynn Gottlieb began her rabbinical studies—the Reform movement had just ordained Sally Priesand as a rabbi, and only a handful of women were at that time enrolled in the rabbinical programs of Hebrew Union College–Jewish Institute of Religion (Reform) and the Reconstructionist Rabbinical College. In response to internal pressure, the Conservative movement had begun formally to consider the issue of women's ordination, but by 1973 the Law Committee of its Rabbinical Assembly voted against such a move. In that same year, the Law Committee did vote to count women in a *minyan* (the quorum of ten necessary for public worship) and gave new emphasis to its little-known 1955 decision granting women *aliyot* (calling them to the Torah) on special occasions. Yet most Conservative congregations in 1973 were hesitant, if not reluctant, to institute such change. Neither the Conservative nor the Reform movement had yet invested women as cantors, and few women in any of Judaism's major movements had yet served as presidents of congregations. Within the Orthodox movement there were a few self-proclaimed feminists as well as a handful of Orthodox rabbis sympathetic to feminist concerns. On the whole, however, Orthodoxy seemed resistant (or oblivious) to feminist demands.

Twenty years later, the Reform, Reconstructionist, and Conservative movements ordain women as rabbis (the Conservative movement having reversed its decision in 1983), and more than two hundred ordained women currently serve as congregational rabbis, hospital chaplains, educators, Hillel directors, and seminary administrators throughout the country. Almost one hundred women have been invested as Reform and Conservative cantors, increasing numbers of Conservative congregations count women in the minyan and regularly give them aliyot, and, outside of Orthodoxy, women now serve on important synagogue committees and as officers of their congregations. Orthodoxy, though still largely resistant to feminist concerns, is no longer oblivious, and increasing numbers of Orthodox rabbis have been forced to acknowledge the growing presence of ongoing women's prayer groups through which Orthodox women—meeting in an all-women setting—have taken on greater roles and responsibilities in communal worship.

As women's demands for equal access to the public sphere of Jewish religious life have increasingly been heard and (outside of Orthodoxy, at least) met, it is all too easy to forget how revolutionary it seemed twenty years ago when Lynn Gottlieb announced her intention to become a rabbi. After leaving the Reform movement's Hebrew Union College–Jewish Institute of Religion (where she briefly studied), she found the Conservative movement's Jewish Theological Seminary unwilling to admit her or any other woman into its rabbinical program. Undaunted, Lynn found a number of Orthodox, Conservative, and Reform rabbis and scholars who were willing to teach her. Thus through both private classes and audited courses (for which she later wrote papers), Lynn continued her intellectual preparation for the rabbinate.

To many within the American Jewish community, Lynn Gottlieb—a female rabbinical student preparing for private ordination—seemed both strange and threatening. The Jewish feminist magazine *Lilith* featured on the cover of its spring/summer 1977 issue a large black-and-white photograph of a smiling Lynn Gottlieb, with a *kippah* on her head and a *tallit* (prayer shawl, which, like the kippah, is traditionally worn only by Jewish men) draped around her shoulders. Emblazoned across the cover was the question, "Why is The Jewish Theological Seminary Afraid of This Woman?" The article focused not on Lynn's personal journey toward ordination but rather on the seminary's refusal to admit women into its rabbinical program. As the *Lilith* cover demonstrated, Lynn had quickly become a symbol of Jewish feminism and of women's increasing demands for equal access within the American Jewish community.

A year later, *Keeping Posted,* the youth magazine of the Reform movement, prominently featured Lynn on its cover as "The New Jewish Woman." Though neither studying for ordination within the Reform movement nor directly pressing for change within the Reform movement itself, Lynn was chosen by the editors of *Keeping Posted* because in many ways she did represent the new Jewish woman: assertive, independent, knowledgeable, and strong. While not yet ordained, and not formally enrolled in a rabbinical program, she had assumed a role of religious leadership as early as 1973, becoming spiritual leader of Temple Beth Or of the Deaf in Queens. In addition, through her three-person performance group, Bat Kol, of which she was a prominent member, Lynn soon began to bring her stories of Jewish women to hundreds, and later thousands, of men and women. By the time *Newsweek* wrote a feature story on Bat Kol in 1977, Lynn had performed before enthusiastic audiences throughout the United States.

In short, by 1977, Lynn Gottlieb had become something of a national Jewish phenomenon. She was known throughout the country because of her work with the deaf (she even appeared on national television), her performance pieces, and the furor that her desire to become a rabbi had caused. Wolfe Kelman, executive vice-president for the Rabbinical Assembly, for example, announced in the *New York Times* that he would ordain Lynn privately if JTS continued to deny women ordination, a statement that some have speculated led the Conservative movement to reopen the issue of women's ordination through the formation of a commission that eventually concluded that women should, in fact, be ordained.

To my mind, Lynn Gottlieb was a symbol of the "new Jewish woman" in more ways than one. During those years in which most Jewish feminists, including myself, focused our energies on gaining greater access to positions of leadership within Jewish religious and communal life, Lynn focused her energies elsewhere. She realized, as most of us have since come to believe, that equal access, though important, is insufficient. What Lynn sought—as early as the 1970s—was nothing less than the transformation of Judaism itself.

Recognizing that institutions can often co-opt us, she chose to work outside an institutional setting. To do so took enormous courage and energy and involved a great deal of risk. Yet knowing Lynn, as I have for almost twenty years, I can honestly say that Lynn could not have acted otherwise. During a time in which feminist historians and theologians were only beginning to talk about the importance of Jewish women reclaiming our voices, Lynn Gottlieb had reclaimed not only her own but also those of our real and imagined foremothers—Lilith and Eve, Rachel and Rebecca, a medieval Spanish Jewess forced to become a "secret Jew," and others. Many of her early performance pieces, like her more recent piece about a Palestinian woman, Um Tahrir, have been highly controversial. Yet Lynn has never been afraid of controversy, for in all of her endeavors, she has been motivated and guided by a religious vision of souls in harmony with themselves, other living beings, and the world in which we live.

Like all religious visionaries who refuse to remain silent, Lynn has been threatened both with physical violence and excommunication (a meaningless threat in today's voluntaristic Jewish community but a hate message nonetheless). She has been sustained by her belief in the truth of her religious message. Drawing on such diverse sources as classical rabbinic texts, including Jewish mystical writings, ancient Near Eastern myths, Native American rituals, and feminist reappropriations of the Goddess, Lynn has attempted not only to tap the spiritual potential of American Jews but also to create a nonsexist, ecologically responsible Jewish peace culture that welcomes into its midst all who seek to become members.

As the prayers, guided meditations, and rituals that Lynn has included in *She Who Dwells Within* so amply demonstrate, Lynn's greatest spiritual gift is her ability to awaken within others an awareness of divine presence, whether that presence be one of immanence or transcendence, of God as Being or God as Power. I have participated in many of Lynn's rituals, celebrated Rosh Hodesh (the New Moon) with her, watched her perform, learned from her teachings, and have sung and danced with many others at her rabbinic ordination. I vividly remember that evening in 1980 when about forty of us, Lynn's friends and family, sat in a large circle in a loft in Greenwich Village and heard Rabbis Everett Gendler and Zalman Schachter-Shalomi confer the title of Rabbi upon her. To those of us who were present, the title was merely a formal confirmation of that which we already knew, namely, that Lynn Gottlieb *was* a rabbi— a teacher and spiritual guide, not just to us but to thousands of American Jews.

In New York—as later in New Mexico—Lynn continued to receive confirmation of her rabbinic calling through communal support. That overwhelming support continues to this day. As I travel throughout the country, I often meet men and women who tell me stories of the ways in which Lynn Gottlieb has led them to reclaim their Jewish heritage, to discover the divine presence, and, perhaps for the first time in their life, to feel at home in the Jewish community. *She Who Dwells Within* invites the reader to share Lynn's courage and commitment to a Judaism that will replenish both our souls and the world with justice, righteousness, and compassion.

Introduction:
What About the Women?

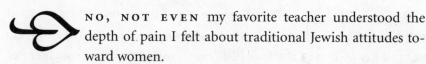

NO, NOT EVEN my favorite teacher understood the depth of pain I felt about traditional Jewish attitudes toward women.

Elie Wiesel strode into a musty classroom at City College of New York, releasing his magic and light. Like kabbalists of old, he could string together soft midnight sounds, and fallen husks of Jewish tradition would suddenly spring to life. My soul yearned for his stories and dreams. Unlike the straightforward teaching styles of other Jewish scholars, Wiesel inspired my artistic imagination. He transformed Hebraic texts into delicate and eternal mysteries. He resonated with tales of ecstatic rabbis and melancholy madmen, of strange meetings and distant places, of the human heart's desperate longing to penetrate the silence of God.

This, my third course with the master, was entitled "Heroes of the Bible." I was poised once again to receive his instruction and revel at his *tish* (table). After greeting us, Wiesel began intoning the names of the biblical heroes he wished us to study. By the time he pronounced the final name, I was crestfallen. His litany included Adam, but not Eve; Cain and Abel, but not their legendary sister; Abraham, but not Sarah or Hagar; Isaac, but not Rebecca; Jacob, but not Rachel, Leah, Bilhah, or Zilpah; Joseph, but not Zuleikah or Asnat; Moses and Aaron, but not Miriam or Yocheved; even Pharaoh, but not his daughter Batya.

My heart pounded in my throat. I raised my hand. He nodded in my direction.

"What about the women?" I ventured.

"Oh, the women. Ah, yes, the women. Why don't you do the women?"

Do the women? Was that the right verb? I felt tongue-tied.

Even though Wiesel did not appear to regard biblical women as equally worthy of his imagination, still, he invited me to "do" the women. I chose Eve.

Following Wiesel's formula for composing our own midrash, I set to work collecting Eve fragments from a wide range of traditional sources. Weaving these together, I shaped a story in answer to a question inspired by my recent contact with Jewish feminism: How might Eve tell her own tale?

When called upon, I offered my version of Eve to the class. I spoke of the first woman's quest for wisdom and her desire to know from the sight of her own eyes, the taste of her own tongue, and the touch of her own hands. I spoke of the courage she summoned to trespass the boundaries imposed on her choices by a man and a God who feared her outreach. I described her initiation into the spirit world by a serpent, who taught her the art of shedding skins. Then I paused. I looked at my teacher's face. How would he respond to my rendition of Eve?

Wiesel smiled, sighed, rolled his eyes, and countered my tale with one of his own. According to my teacher, woman's basic gullibility doomed her to exile from the garden. As Wiesel told the story, Eve found herself alone one afternoon for the first time after Adam strolled off some-where. Drawing on traditional commentary, Wiesel related how the snake took the opportunity to seduce Eve, using her own words, into eating the forbidden fruit. Alas, conjectured Wiesel, if only Adam had stayed at home to supervise his foolish wife. She wouldn't have gotten herself and the rest of humanity into so much trouble. When Adam finally returned from his adventure, Eve cried until her befuddled husband ate the forbidden fruit as well. "And who can refuse a tearful wife?" quipped Wiesel. "Anyway, no tragedy is complete without a woman."

I gazed into Wiesel's soft, pensive eyes. For all his powers of imagination he could not think beyond the weary stereotypes of women so endlessly repeated in Jewish literature. Elie Wiesel's version of Eve was informed by the same age-old opinions Jewish men have carried around for millennia; that is, men are smarter and more important than women but are easily seduced by their dangerous wiles. As Samson Raphael Hirsh wrote in the nineteenth century in *Judaism Eternal,* "The male sex is the depository of the Divine revelations and the spiritual attainments of the human race. . . . The man chooses a calling, creates a position for himself, the woman receives both by attaching herself to a man, entering his calling and his position." Maybe women could sit beside Wiesel in synagogue or even read Torah in his presence, but change the way women are presented in the stories? This, apparently, was not permitted.

Perhaps it was unrealistic to expect Wiesel to take to heart a feminist point of view as early as 1977. After all, since the beginnings of Jewish history most of the official interpreters of Jewish religion have been men. Men have recorded their laws, commentaries, legends, prayers, theologies, mystical testimonies, and politics in thousands upon thousands of volumes. Until recently women's words have not found life on the written page. Men have acted on the assumption that they, and not women, were the ultimate authorities in both the public and the private domain.

Although Jewish men did not, as some feminists claim, invent the system of male domination known as "patriarchy," they perpetuated the exclusion of women from the priesthood, the rabbinate, and from religious discipleship and secular leadership within the Jewish community. Only a few women broke through these constraints and sought expression of their ideas and work in the public domain. The result has been an overwhelming absence of women's voices in Jewish texts and a dearth of women communal leaders and teachers.

Women have had little say. Our fathers, uncles, brothers, husbands, and a host of male authorities have controlled the scope of our activities. Our names have been unrecorded, glossed over, or suppressed. Our contributions have been devalued or forgotten. Our choices have been mostly limited to the domestic sphere.

This attitude toward Jewish women's role in life was recently reiterated by several Orthodox rabbis in Israel in response to women who wished to pray together as a group at the Western Wall. According to Jewish law, only ten *men* can make up a prayer quorum (minyan) for public worship. Even though the women were extremely careful not to act like a minyan (omitting, for instance, certain prayers), their actions were viewed with horror by the Israeli religious establishment. Rabbi Shlomo Goren, the former chief Ashkenazi rabbi wrote,

> When women create their own congregations, the *Shekinah* is not present and their prayers are not heard. . . . Instead of *kedush* [holiness], we have *kedaysha* [prostitution]. Never have we heard, never have we seen anything as strange as this since the time of Moses our Rabbi until today. Not even Reform Jews would have conceived of such a thing. The women have created this by drawing upon an unclean source called "women's lib" whose purpose is to overturn the words of the living God!

Rabbi Moshe Feinstein commented, "Women who are stubborn and who wish to fight and to make changes are considered heretics who do not have a share in the world to come."

Rabbi Menashe Klein had this to say:

> These women who rush to create their own groups and who form minyans also do everything to bar conception from taking place. God should save us from this. From their use of birth control we

see that their motivation is not for the sake of heaven and that they run after that which is forbidden. . . . They neglect their husbands which is why they were created. [*sic!*][1]

Admittedly these rabbis represent the most regressive thinking about Jewish women in our time, but their influence is considerable, and they perpetuate what was mainstream opinion less than fifty years ago. Their attitudes are reflected in normative Jewish theology, legend, custom, mores, and law.

Where traditional faith has been replaced by secular beliefs, Jewish women still find themselves pressured to limit their community involvement to the nurturing roles. As Suzannah Heschel observes, "Even as traditional beliefs concerning God and revelation were abandoned, traditional role distinctions and definitions of femaleness were not eliminated, but simply given new expression."[2]

In the past century we have witnessed a revolution in women's expectations. A young Jewish garment worker named Mollie Schepps articulated this sentiment when she addressed a crowd gathered at New York's Cooper Union in the spring of 1912 on behalf of women's right to vote. "As we [women] are not angels, nor are they [men] Gods. We are simply in business together and as such, we refuse to play the silent partner any longer."[3]

Since the advent of the twentieth century, Jewish women have been steadily moving from silence and submission toward women's liberation. We are breaking down the barriers that restricted our lives and are empowering ourselves to refashion a tradition based on the assumption of our equality. Not as separate but equal, but as fully able and equal. Feminism, the movement for women's rights, has confirmed our recent perceptions that Jewish women have, indeed, been an oppressed class within our culture. We have been denied the material, legal, and spiritual privileges granted to the group of people we have been required to serve, that is, men.

Along with the denial of privileges came systems of justification for our lower status. The use of negative stereotyping concomitant with a stress on certain behaviors as normative, the denial of education, the weight of rabbinic tradition, economic dependency, and physical and sexual harassment—all have served to curtail our life choices.

Women need a new situation. In a Jewish context, we need to transform the way we talk Torah, the way we practice ceremony and ritual, the way we tell and pass on stories, the way we codify laws, the way we organize our communities, and the way we envision sacred mysteries. We need to reinterpret the spiritual paradigms of our people so that they affirm a positive and expanded understanding of what it means to be a Jewish woman. As we go about this process, male authorities can no longer negate women's perceptions and writings with the words "but Judaism says" or "according to the sages," because women were not part of such formulations. We cannot be expected to abide by norms we did not help to create.

The urge to craft a Judaism that nourishes both women and men motivated the writing of *She Who Dwells Within*. It is meant as a practical guide to nonsexist Judaism. The phrase "She Who Dwells Within" is translated from the Hebrew word *Shekinah*, which refers to the female presence of God in Jewish tradition. Since the medieval period, Jewish mystics and storytellers have envisioned God as a combination of masculine and feminine forces. Shekinah, or She Who Dwells Within, came to represent Jewish longing for an end to exile. Although all the descriptions of Shekinah were written by men, Her very existence in Jewish lore legitimizes the right of women to write about religious experience through the language of feminine metaphor.

She Who Dwells Within: A Feminist Vision of a Renewed Judaism speaks to the longing for a Judaism that welcomes the creativity of women in all arenas of Jewish expression. Just as Shekinah has been in exile, so Jewish women have been in exile. Our exile, however, has been in the midst of our own culture. Denied access to avenues of public expression, we were denied the ability to shape Jewish culture explicitly. This is the exile *She Who Dwells Within* seeks to end.

I have identified four basic components of Jewish culture and have used them to form the internal division of the book: theology, story, ceremony, and community. The first part on theology begins with my first encounter with "the Goddess," moves through a brief history of Shekinah in Jewish sources, and then explores three traditional images of Shekinah from a feminist perspective: Shekinah as the Being Who Connects All Life, Shekinah as the Longing for Wholeness, and Shekinah as the Cry for Justice.

The theology offered in part 1 works with a midrashic or storyteller's reinterpretation of metaphors rather than offering an explicit account of the nature of God as one finds in much of the kabbala. In that sense, I do not follow the recent penchant to place Jewish mysticism as the principal way into Jewish spirituality and theology. Instead I rely on women's stories, poems, prayers, and archaeology as well as Jewish legends as sources for reimaging the Mystery.

The second part works with the much overlooked and devalued women's story and song traditions within Jewish culture. Women's oral traditions, including women's drum and song traditions recorded in the Bible along with more recently collected tales often categorized as "folklore," serve as springboards for the retelling of core biblical tales about women. This part begins with my personal discovery of the importance of women's interpretive traditions and proceeds with stories grouped into three sections: "Primeval Ancestors," "Tribal Mothers," and "The Freedom Generation."

"Primeval Ancestors" restores the prebiblical archetype of a female Creatrix to contemporary Jewish liturgy. Tehomot or Tiamat, the name of the Creatrix in the Mesopotamian myth that inspired the first creation story of Genesis, and Shekinah are remythologized in prayers and stories that can be incorporated into the body of Jewish liturgy.

Next, Lilith, an ancient goddess representing the destructive side of creation who found her way into Jewish legend as the ultimate evil woman, is reconsidered in the light of feminism.

Finally, I present the life of Eve, no longer regarded as sinful. Eve is recast as "everywoman" on the journey through girlhood, middle years, and old age. The division of Eve's life into three stages reflects her roots as an archetype for the cyclical nature of life so often represented by the tripartite goddess. The inverted triangle is also a sign for the tripartite goddesses of the ancient Near East. It symbolizes the vagina and the womb and the corridor to the mysteries of birth and death. Eve is the mythic persona in Jewish tradition who carries the remnants of women's prebiblical religion, which imaged the divine as a changing woman.

One of the greatest challenges for Jewish women is the broadening of religious meaning around the telling of the stories of our first "Tribal Mothers," Sarah, Hagar, Rebecca, Rachel, and Leah. These women (with the exception of Hagar, who is honored by women in Muslim traditions) have served as spiritual role models for generations of Jewish women. On Friday evening girls are told, "May you be like Sarah and Rebecca, Rachel and Leah," after their mothers light the candles. Yet the lives of these women are told only in relationship to husbands and sons. We do not hear about their birth, even in legend, nor about their lives once their sons become men. "Tribal Mothers" both honors these women as matriarchs of our people and extends the story of their lives so that they affirm women-to-women relationships as well.

"The Freedom Generation" retells the stories of the midwives, Serach Bat Asher, Shifra, Yocheved, and Miriam. These women appear in the Bible and Jewish legend as heroines in the drama of the Israelite exodus from the slavery of Egypt. Although their stories are fuller than those of most women of the Bible, they still have not found their way into the liturgy of Passover. I would like to retell the stories of these women so they can become a standard feature of Judaism's most celebrated holy day. As we struggle to liberate our tradition from the bonds of sexism, may these women's stories help us envision our freedom.

Part 3 offers ceremonies that affirm women's lives. Jewish women's ceremonial history includes rituals and customs that women created around birth and pregnancy, weaning, the onset of menstruation, marriage and death, and holy day celebrations, including Rosh Hodesh. Male authorities often regarded these customs and rituals with suspicion, seeing them as too pagan rather than as a natural Jewish response to life-cycle occasions. This part is meant to help us honor women's ceremonial history as well as to encourage women to create ceremony for the events in our lives today.

I begin with the Mishkan ceremony, which I composed as a personal prayer and healing ritual for women. It is based on the mythic image of the Mishkan, or wilderness shrine, built by the Israelites to be a dwelling place for God's presence. The Mishkan housed a sacred object in each of the four directions: the altar in the east, the seven-branched menorah in the south, the stone tablets in the west, and the twelve loaves of offering in the north. Each of these symbols has roots in the early biblical religious practice of building shrines to the Goddess, which contained her symbolic icons.

Over time, public shrines to the Goddess gave way to a temple to God. Nonetheless, women continued to set up private altars in their homes as a way of expressing their need to connect through the symbols of their daily lives to a feminine Presence. This is the essence of the ritual around the Sabbath table wherein the use of candles, braided bread, and the liturgical image of the Sabbath Queen and Bride link Jewish women on an intuitive, if not explicit, level to the feminine divine. The Mishkan ceremony restores our awareness of the Goddess nature of the symbols associated with the tabernacle and reintroduces them as sources for prayer and ritual.

Ceremony also provides a "recipe" for the celebration of the New Moon, or Rosh Hodesh, which has been known as a woman's holy day for over three thousand years. Rosh Hodesh has become a time for contemporary women to explore the connection between feminism and Judaism and to learn about Jewish women's history and custom in an all-women setting. I have suggested twelve themes for each of the new moons and an order of service to help women initiate Rosh Hodesh groups in their own communities.

Part 3 closes with a series of rituals for the initiation of young Jewish women into their womanhood, a prayer for mothers, and two ceremonies honoring elder women. Although not complete in its scope, this part will, I hope, provide women with inspiration to create the rituals they need to honor their own lives.

The fourth part, "Community," envisions a more ecologically oriented Judaism, one that transforms the trauma of the Holocaust into a quest for reconciliation with the Palestinian people, and one that is based on egalitarian relationships between men and women. Part 4 also includes a series of ceremonies designed to heal the wounds of sexual abuse and violence and offers practical suggestions for action in pursuit of justice and reconciliation.

The comprehensive structure of *She Who Dwells Within* is based on the traditional organization of Jewish codes of law, which often included theology, Torah interpretation, holy day commentary, prayers, stories, and personal reflections in one work. In addition, an account of my own journey as a woman rabbi is woven throughout the text so it may serve as one woman's witness to dramatically changing times.

Since the fall of 1972, when I commenced my rabbinic training, more than two hundred women (as part of a pool of six thousand men) have entered the rabbinate. The appearance of women rabbis has been accompanied by changes in prayer language and the introduction of new rituals to meet neglected life-cycle needs. A growing body of feminist scholarly and artistic work is replacing the standard "victim mentality," which perpetuates us-versus-them polarizations, with a process of reconciliation between peers who learn to listen and respond. I feel hopeful that this process will continue.

My struggle with Elie Wiesel occurred more than eighteen years ago. Now women's right to a nonsexist Judaism is finally being acknowledged by ourselves and men as a legitimate mainstream endeavor.

There is still much work ahead as we continue to involve the next generation in the accomplishments of the preceding one and to inspire them to carry forth the work.

I would like to conclude this introduction by affirming my love of Jewish people and culture despite revelations of our sexism. We are a four-thousand-year-old people who have much to preserve as well as much to change. In particular, I would like to give thanks to the thousands of Jewish women and men who remain committed to the creation of a nonsexist Judaism. I also give honor to all the people who persist in their dedication to the work of justice and beauty in order to make the world a better place for all the world's children.

Part One

☙ THEOLOGY

Yehudim: Unifications

Shekinah is the consuming fire
By which dreamers are renewed at night.
This fire takes all souls unto itself
And encloses them in its flame.

Shekinah is the great wide place
Which contains everything
Yet is not filled.
As it is written:
All rivers flow to the sea;
The sea takes them in
Brings them forth anew
And they go their way.
Amen, amen.

There is no place devoid of Shekinah.
The whole earth is full of her glory.
This is the face of Shekinah:
Ancestor spirits,
Angels and the ones who inhabit unseen worlds,
The body of Israel,
Torah Sheh B'al Peh.
All these are sustained by Her light.

Shekinah is the womb of emanations,
Great Mother Binah,
Replete with understanding.
Her wisdom gives order and pattern to the living.
Daughters and sons She bears without number.
We are the fibers of Her being.
In Her great round
Time is born.
Between the mystery of beginnings and our return
We travel Her way.

(Adapted from the kabbala and Goddess sources)

1

The Forbidden Fruits of Winter 1975

I REMEMBER the first time She called me. I was hunched over the Talmudic tractate called Ketubot (Marriage Contracts) in the Jewish Theological Seminary library, trying to decipher rabbinic conversations about girls not yet menstruating who must engage in sexual intercourse to consummate a marriage. How soon after the first time may intercourse be repeated? After four days, says one. Till the wound heals, says another. Not until the following Shabbat, counters yet another rabbinic sage. I once asked Dr. Francus, who graciously let me attend his class in Talmud when no women were as yet admitted to JTS's rabbinic program, whether he thought the sages consulted women on this subject. He stared at me blankly.

I glanced hopefully out the window. Twilight tinged the horizons, heralding the hour of my release. I swept up the heavy volumes of rabbinic commentary and sailed down the stairs out into the city. A modern sculpture of the burning bush suspended over the entrance to the seminary declared words of revelation: "And the bush was not consumed." Yellow and red city lights cloaked the iron leaves in a thick urban haze. I swung around, inhaled deeply, and set out toward Union Theological Seminary, where the New York Feminist Scholars in Religion were meeting to discuss their personal relationship with the Goddess. My anxiety level soared. A battery of biblical taboos pounded in my head. "You shall have no other gods before Me! Don't even try to find out about other gods. The practices of other nations are perversions."

Yet just as the biblical character Dinah ventured forth, I felt compelled to "go out and meet the women of the land," even though I feared the encounter. I found myself opposite the granite towers of Union Theological Seminary, which stands like a medieval castle on the banks of the Hudson River. I skirted the main entrance and hurried to the north side of the building, where other members of the group clustered around a small wooden door like bees at a hive. Bev Harrison, a Christian feminist and professor of theology at Union, ushered us into a lounge, where we sipped tea and chatted.

When Bev called us to order, the familiar pounding heart thundered inside me. The all-woman group was composed of the vanguard of Christian and post-Christian feminist scholars and three Jews: Ellen Umansky, Judith Plaskow, and myself. I, the fledgling feminist, asked myself what I was doing there.

Carol Christ in particular epitomized my notion of the post-Christian pagan woman. Tall, blond, and beautiful, Carol resembled the nude statue of the Goddess Diana in the Metropolitan Museum. Sinewy and graceful, Diana aims her arrow with precision, her nakedness untamed and free, like the virgin forests she inhabits. Carol similarly evoked a physical and psychic freedom that both excited and panicked me.

That evening Carol spoke lovingly of the Goddess in her life and the reasons she needed her. She had rejected God for the Goddess.

I resisted and scurried into an imaginative corner, where the aged Dr. Elk reminded me that the righteous Abraham smashed his father's idols, and Rachel died for hiding female statues under her skirts. Clothed in his faded brown suit, submerged in leather-bound books stacked in formless piles against the walls of his tiny, windowless office in Haifa, Dr. Elk waved a Bible in our faces and told us to open our texts to the first page. I was one of his pupils in 1966, when I spent seven months in Israel as a high school exchange student.

"Genesis, chapter one, was written in order to demythologize the gods of the ancient Near East. In the Bible, gods and goddess are reduced to natural phenomena under the control of God." He gave us the example of Tiamat, who appears in the Assyrian creation tale as mother of the gods and the fearsome opponent of the sun god, Marduk. In Genesis she is converted into the primordial abyss called Tehom. Dr. Elk taught us that unlike Asherah, El, Baal, Mot, and Anat, the gods of the Canaanites, YHVH Elohim did not fight or fornicate. He had no opponents, because He was the one true transcendent being. Dr. Elk viewed paganism as a primitive and superstitious religion and Judaism as rational and prophetic. Pagans were slaves to the whims of childish gods, while the Israelites could depend on YHVH's consistency. Paganism promoted lewdness, while Judaism upheld moral conduct; pagans were chained to endlessly repetitive cycles of nature, while the Israelites were freed by YHVH's redemptive character to enter history.

I looked at Carol and realized I had missed most of her conversation.

Sheila Collins, who was present that evening, represented for me at the time those feminists who accuse the ancient Hebrews of dismantling Goddess religions. I am still troubled by the persistence of this belief among many feminists.

Sheila's portrayal of Jews in her book *A Different Heaven and Earth*, intimates theacide by the Hebrews and echoes the traditional Christian polemic that the Jews murdered Jesus. This perspective had caused much resentment between the Jewish and Christian women at the previous meeting, and it had not yet been resolved. Sheila's view of early

Judaism placed another barrier in my path toward experiencing the Goddess.

Other women in the group identified Christianity as a natural context for their experience of the Goddess through the figure of Mary. I reasoned to myself that it wasn't much of a leap for a Christian woman to experience the Goddess since the concept of the Trinity and the existence of Mary, Mother of God, already opened them to a multidimensional Godhead. Jewish monotheism, however, seemed to preclude incarnate images of the divine.

Then Ann Barstow spoke. For some reason I was not agitated or intimidated by her presence. She recounted her trip to Catal Hüyük in Turkey, which is the Neolithic site of a shrine to a goddess. Ann wrote about her experience in *The Book of the Goddess,* where she says, "I was incredibly affirmed as a woman standing before Her. She was immense, larger than life, carved in stone, towering over rows of breasts and bull horns, legs stretched wide, giving birth."

What would the Talmudic sages say about Her? I challenged Ann, but my voice did not seem my own. Why did an oversized statue with breasts affirm her womanhood? Ann answered me patiently, as if she knew my fear, having heard it many times before.

Seeing her own body represented as the body of the Creator caused her to experience the numinous nature of her physical and spiritual being. Instead of shame, she felt pride in her womanhood. Women's ability to give birth symbolized the creative process of the divine.

Did She whisper to me then? She said, "My body is the mountain, My birth waters are the parting seas. Speak these words, and you will not be consumed." What if I permitted other words, other images, of God? What if I imagined YHVH as a woman giving birth? The rabbinic sages record a folk legend that describes the God witnessed by the Israelites at the shores of the Red Sea as a man of war, and the God of Sinai as a learned sage. What if I replaced the Man of War with a Woman Giving Birth?

Yes. This seemed right. I was already publicly performing the story of Miriam and the midwives and highlighting the birth images inherent in the story to emphasize the divine activity of freeing a people. Why not see YHVH as She Who Gives Birth to Her People?

YHVH Giving Birth

YHVH giving birth
At the shores of the Red Sea
Squatting over the waters
Spreading her legs wide.
Women dancing in the salt sea waters
Midwives at Her occasion
YHVH's birth cries
Sounds of jubilation
As a people is born.
YHVH midwife woman
With strong arms and outstretched hands
Opening Her womb,
Giving birth to freedom.

Later, after bidding my colleagues and friends good-bye, I descended into the dark passages of Manhattan's underground. In the steady screech and rumble of the subway, I heard my own small voice whispering inside me. Yes, I need the Goddess. I need her to midwife the spirit that sings with a woman's voice inside me.

2
A Brief History of Shekinah,
She Who Dwells Within

"God is always referred to as 'He' in the masculine gender.
The feminine gender is not used because God
is an active force in the universe."

Aryeh Kaplan, *The Handbook of Jewish Thought*

THE POETIC IMAGE of YHVH giving birth satisfied a hunger I had not been consciously aware of. Still, could a Jewish God become a woman giving birth? Was it really possible to pray to a feminine YHVH? Could "She" authentically be part of a religion that seemed to allow only the masculine metaphor?

Soon after my acknowledgment of the need to seek the feminine face of God, I was introduced to kabbalistic and hasidic texts by members of the New York and Boston Havurot (a religious community of peers). Lo

19

and behold! The "Goddess" was alive and well in the midst of my own tradition.

As it is written in the twelfth-century mystical text known as the Zohar, "Thou shalt have no other gods before Me. Said R. Isaac, 'This prohibition of other gods does not include the Shekinah'" (Zohar 86a).

Shekinah, the feminine Presence of God, is a central metaphor of divinity in Jewish mystical and midrashic texts from the first millennium C.E. onward. I was amazed to discover this focus on the feminine divine when I began to read the texts myself. I felt like an orphan who uncovered documents that proved her mother was not dead. All the ambivalence about "God She" was replaced with the fervor of an explorer who has just been given the right treasure map.

I plunged into the stacks of the Jewish Theological Seminary library and began hounding my teachers for information about my newly discovered relative. Who was She? Where did She live? Would She speak to me in a language I could understand?

What I found was both inspiring and disappointing. To begin with, everything written about the Shekinah appears to have been authored by men. Women's relationship to the Shekinah is nowhere recorded. Yet much of the material about the Shekinah seems to draw from that vast wellspring of the human unconscious that formulates images in archetypes even as it draws upon specific cultural influences.

The idea of Shekinah in Jewish tradition testifies to the basic human impulse to express the experience of the numinous through symbols that include the "feminine." Kabbalistic works that describe the Shekinah may incorporate aspects of women's experience in implicit ways. Without women's voices interpreting and composing Shekinah texts for themselves, however, we can never fully grasp women's experience of the divine.

The term *Shekinah* is an abstract noun of feminine gender derived from the Hebrew root *Sh-Kh-N*, meaning "to dwell" or "to abide." The word *Shekinah* first appears in the Mishnah and Talmud (ca. 200 C.E.), where it is used interchangeably with YHVH and Elohim as names of God. Shekinah evolved from the word *Mishkan,* which refers to the tent the Israelites constructed in the wilderness to house the altar, the seven-branched menorah, the stone tablets, and the twelve loaves of bread baked as an offering to God. After the Israelites received the Torah, they were instructed to build the Mishkan, "So I can dwell among you." When the shrine was completed, YHVH appeared to the people as a cloud of light indicating His Presence.

The destruction of the first Temple in Jerusalem in 586 B.C.E. by the Babylonians resulted in the first exile of the Jewish people and engendered a crisis of faith. The Israelites wondered whether God's Presence, which had previously dwelled in the Temple, would continue to abide in their exile. Ultimately that concern was answered in the affirmative. God's abiding Presence, formerly represented as a cloud of glory, became known as the Shekinah. The Shekinah was said to accompany the people into exile and would appear to them whenever the people occupied themselves with the study of Torah or performed good deeds. Although the Temple was destroyed, ritual and the behavior of the people became the new dwelling place for God's Presence.

Over time, the biblical themes of exile and redemption and the historical experience of the Jewish people under Roman and Christian Europe continued to shape the meaning of Shekinah. Women's role as professional mourners and the midrashic image of Israel as God's marriage partner were particularly influential in the evolution of Shekinah into a feminine aspect of God. By 1000 C.E., the very mythologies so suppressed in the Bible erupted in the heart of Jewish mysticism, known as the kabbala, and Shekinah became YHVH's wife, lover, and daughter.

Kabbalists conceive of God in Neoplatonic terms, as a dynamic complex of ten energies or spheres that emanate from a hidden and unknowable Source. The whole system is known as the Tree of Life. The divine spheres represent the hidden and inner life of God, which becomes manifest in the material world of existence through the medium of the Shekinah. However, the Shekinah occupies the bottom rung of the hierarchical chain of divine emanations.

Although the kabbala spawned a multitude of descriptions of the divine, the qualities ascribed to male and female spheres remained constant. In the kabbala the feminine is always helpless and dependent, not able to act upon the world. The maleness of God is linked to the upper worlds, God's active intellect, the positive commandments, the initiating and redemptive forces of divine will, and with compassion. The feminine side of God is linked to the material world, the negative commandments, stern judgment, the side of evil, passivity, and exile. Shekinah is the passive and receptive aspect of the divine, unable to generate her own light, incapable of enacting her own redemption, and never the subject of petitionary prayer. Shekinah is the fairy-tale princess locked in a tower or abandoned in the streets, waiting for her mystic prince to rescue her and restore her, through marriage, to her true position. Shekinah's salvation depends on male acts of courage and spiritual bravery.

The hierarchical division of male and female gender traits in Jewish mysticism mirrored earthly arrangements between men and women. In many ways Shekinah embodied male projections of women as overly emotional, earthbound, and sexually dangerous beings. Nonetheless, not all the figurative language associated with the Shekinah is negative. In fact many of the descriptions of the Shekinah in Jewish sources hark back to images that once belonged to the ancient goddesses of the Near East. Waxing and waning moon, evening and morning star, mirror, well of waters, primordial sea, rose amid the thorns, lily of the valley, Mother Wisdom, the oral tradition of Torah, Womb of Emanations, gateway and door, house and sacred shrine, doe, dove, mother eagle, serpent, the soul of women ancestors, the community of Israel, the Sabbath Queen and Bride, the Tree of Life, the menorah, and the earth itself all belong to the poetic constellation of the Shekinah. These images will be explored in more detail throughout this book.

The many images associated with the Shekinah can become a source for women's encounter with the divine today as well as a bridge to our past. Women yearn for this possibility. When women speak of God She, we can finally picture ourselves created in God's image. One incident stands out in my mind as an illustration of the need for an expansive, figurative language for God based in feminine language.

About seventeen years ago I led a retreat for a Reform congregation in Chicago. During morning services I substituted the word *Shekinah* for *Adonai* and spoke of Shekinah as Midwife Woman. After services a woman whose husband was active in the Reform movement confessed her alienation from traditional prayer language. With tears in her eyes, surprised at her own outpouring, she admitted that this was the first time in years that she could relate to Jewish prayer. Speaking the name Shekinah in place of Adonai released within her the ability to experience God. No longer "the other," she suddenly found herself in the center of theological metaphors.

This kind of response to feminine prayer language, story, and ceremony has been repeated hundreds of times in my presence throughout the last twenty years. If language is a gateway to the Ineffable, then women need linguistic passage to that realm. Speaking the Word as Shekinah allows us to traverse that way.

Toward this goal, the next three chapters are devoted to crafting theological language that draws upon both traditional images of Shekinah and my own understanding of those images from a feminist point of view.

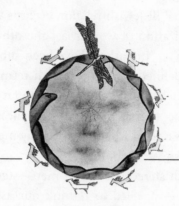

3
Shekinah as the Being Who Connects All Life

The Shema is the central prayer of Jewish faith:

Shema, Yisrael, YHVH Elohanu, YHVH Echad.
Hear, O Israel, YHVH is our God, YHVH is One.

JEWS RECITE these words three times daily: at dawn, at dusk, and before sleeping and as the last words before death. They testify to the Jewish belief in the essential unity of the cosmos, creation as a vast embrace. Jewish teachings rest on the perception that the forces of creation, destruction, and regeneration form a whole pattern of being. That which appears distinct and separate actually exists as part of an interdependent network. As it is written: "Who forms light and creates darkness, who makes *shalom* [harmony] and creates the whole" (from the morning prayer based on Isaiah).

The Shema warns us not to objectify any part of life and urges us to treat all life as a creation of the Sacred Mystery. It is therefore to be cherished and protected. Jewish religious practice is dedicated to seeing and honoring the unity of life while celebrating the uniqueness of every created being.

This particular goal of Jewish religion accords with the feminist goal of ending the polarization of women as "the other." Sexism thrives on stereotypes. Women as "the other" have been subjected to centuries of depersonalization, defined not on our own terms but by a given culture's designated roles and by judgments about what are or are not appropriate "feminine" characteristics. Assertiveness in women, for example, has been seen as a flaw; when practiced by men, however, assertiveness is deemed a positive attribute.

In order to banish stereotypes of women—stereotypes we ourselves have often believed—we need to rethink our associations with those characteristics. In this way we will be able to embrace our uniqueness more fully and to realize a more authentic self.

An important step toward this goal is to break free of language that inhibits women's ability to see God in ourselves. Imaging the Mystery through the language of Shekinah is one way to do this, and I offer prayers in this chapter to that end.

Some people might question the need to rely on gender imagery in the service of prayer altogether. Many contemporary Jewish liturgists argue that God should be addressed in neutral language. "He" is replaced with "You," King with Ruler or Creator, and Father, Parent. That way one can keep the traditional prayer structure with only minor alterations. However, these prayers still echo the hierarchical images embedded in traditional phraseology in which God is He. Altering a noun or pronoun does not change the basic images of the maleness of God in the prayer. In creating prayers for nonsexist Judaism, I want to be free to say God She.

PRAYERS NAMING SHEKINAH

A Meditation on the Feminine Nature of Shekinah

Shekinah is She Who Dwells Within,
The force that binds and patterns creation.

She is Birdwoman, Dragonlady, Queen of the Heavens,
Opener of the Way.
She is Mother of the Spiritworld, Morning and Evening
   Star,
Dawn and Dusk.
She is Mistress of the Seas, Tree of Life,
Silvery Moon, Fiery Sun.
All these are Her names.
Shekinah is Changing Woman, Nature herself,
Her own Law and Mystery.
She is cosmos, dark hole, fiery moment of beginning.
She is dust cloud, nebulae, the swirl of galaxies.
She is gravity, magnetic field,
the paradox of waves and particles.
Shekinah is unseen dark, invisible web,
Creatrix of complex systems,
expanding, contracting, spiraling, meandering,
The beginning of Wisdom.
Shekinah is Grandmother, Grandfather,
   Unborn Child.
Shekinah is life loving itself into being.
Shekinah is the eros of life, limitless desire,
Cosmic orgasm, wave upon wave of arousal,
hungry and tireless, explosive and seductive,
the kiss of life and death, never dying.
Shekinah is home and hearth, root and rug,
the altar on which we light our candles.
We live here, in Her body.
She feeds multitudes from Her flesh,

Water, sap, blood, milk, fluids of life, elixir of
    the wounded.
Shekinah is the catalyst of our passion,
Our inner Spiritfire, our knowledge of self-worth,
Our call to authenticity.
She warms our hearts, ignites our vision.
She is the great turning round,
breathing and pulsating, pushing life toward
    illumination.
Womb and Grave, End and Beginning.
All these are her names.

Psalms are a vital component of traditional worship. As prayer-poems in praise of the Spirit of Life, they serve as vehicles through which we offer our honor and adoration. This one is adapted from a psalm to Ishtar. Many psalms in the Torah were adapted from Canaanite literature and transformed into hymns for YHVH. I have also borrowed from Near Eastern literary images for the divine, but instead of YHVH as storm god, I present Shekinah as feminine Creator.

This psalm can be used as part of Friday evening liturgy to welcome the Sabbath. The Sabbath is often portrayed as a Bride or a Queen in traditional sources. Women are honored before the Sabbath meal with a text from Proverbs known as Eshet Hayil, or a woman of virtue, and a recitation from the Song of Songs. The persona of the Sabbath Bride is honored through the praise of women as part of the ceremony of this holy day. The following psalm returns the feminine persona of the Sabbath to her root in the Goddess.

✑ *A Psalm in Praise of the Shekinah for Shabbat*

Praise Her,
    most awesome of the mighty!
Revere Her,

She is a woman of the people.
Adore Her,
  She is clothed in love.
Laden with vitality,
  Her lips are sweet.
Life is in Her mouth.
When we see Her,
  our rejoicing becomes full.
She is glorious;
  She is beautiful.
Her eyes glisten like the morning star;
  Her face shines like the sun.
Her hair shimmers like the golden moon.
She is a woman of the people;
  with Her is their counsel.
The fate of all the living She holds in Her hands;
  She protects the day and guards the night.
She opens the heavens to life,
  the earth to seed and flower.
She is all women—
  Virgin, Mother, Crone,
  Creator and Peacemaker,
  Servant and Consecrator of Wisdom.
She keeps the hearth fires bright
  and heals the soul of Her people.
Power is in Her hands;
  compassion is in Her heart.
Praise Her when you come upon Her name:
  Tehom, Coiled Serpent Woman;

Elat Hashachan, She Who Ascends with the Dawn;
Shaddai, Many-breasted Woman,
    Whose milk overflows;
Achoti Calah, Sister Whole unto Herself;
Em Ham'rachemet, Mother Whose Womb Is
    Compassion;
Malchat Shamayim, Woman of the Endless Skies;
Dayenet HaEmet, Seal of Truth;
Yehoyah, Spiritwind Woman;
Elohim, SheHe in Love with Life;
Shekinah, Beloved Friend.
She is the breath of all living;
    wild horses dance round Her moon.
Power is in Her hands,
    love is in Her heart.
Praise Her
    when you come upon Her name
    singing inside you
Y'la la la la la la la la la la la la

TWO DAWN PRAYERS FOR
THE MORNING RITUAL

Since ancient times, the morning star has been associated with Near Eastern goddesses, in particular, Inanna/Ishtar. In Jewish tradition the biblical heroine Esther was also known as the dawn star. The star heralds the beginning of a new day and marks the time of morning prayers.

The first prayer for the dawn is a meditation on the attributes of Shekinah associated with hearth and fire culled from kabbalistic sources. The second prayer was inspired by a piece of Canaanite pottery depicting two women washing each other's hands.

In Jewish tradition the first ritual act upon rising is the washing of hands to consecrate our actions in the service of Shekinah. The first prayer is said after the washing of hands, as you offer morning prayers before your home altar, known as the Mishkan.

The second prayer is said at dawn facing the morning star after you light incense on your home altar.

Prayer to Shekinah, Eternal Fire

Shekinah, Olat Tamid,
You are the Eternal Fire
We kindle anew each morning
Upon the altar in our home.
Shekinah, Hearth Fire of creation,
Earth and heart,
Flame bursting forth,
Exploding like the dawn.
Shekinah, Chai Olamim,
Eternal Vitality,
Only appears dead.
Possum Woman
Rolls over, then gets up.
She throws Her head back laughing,
because She revives from instant to instant.
Shekinah, Makor Hayim,
Digging wells,
Drawing water from the depths,
Spawning myriads in her mud,
Frog eggs on a slimy string.
Shekinah, Makom,

Place of the World,
Her sovereignty is the seal of creation.

Greeting Shekinah

Two figures face each other,
Sitting close to the earth in the old way;
Outside in the early morn
The women face each other,
Eye to eye, smile to smile,
Squatting over the earth,
Backs curved like earthen pots.
So gracefully they sit,
Pouring water over each other's hands.
Fire pales as the sun rises;
The spice of dew consecrates the hour
"Shekinah of the sun, Shekinah of the moon,
We greet You with our morning song,
We greet You with the washing of hands,
We greet You with our dawn fire.
Shekinah of the morning star, Shekinah of the dew,
We welcome You as the running deer,
Our feet swift in dancing.
We welcome You as the golden eagle,
Our hands spread in prayer.
We welcome You as the shimmering stream,
Our spirit flowing to the sea of Your delight.
We bless the day with our rising smoke.
Let our prayers ascend to the skies.

Let our prayers touch the earth.

Shalom Achoti, shalom Sister,

All life sings Your song.

Shema Yisrael: Meditation in the Language of Shekinah

Shema, be attentive to this!

Yisrael, you who walk the Spiritpath,

Shekinah, the Being One,

Elohanu, All Spirits,

Shekinah, the Being One,

Echad, embraces all being.

To what does "embraces all being" compare? It is like the Persian story of *The Conference of the Birds:* A long time ago, when animals could talk, a golden feather fell to earth somewhere in China. Word of this miraculous event spread across the land, and birds of every feather gathered to decide what to do. Led by the wise hopoe, the colorful little bird who flies with the queen of Sheba, all the birds agreed to set out for the palace of the Great Simurg, to whom the feather belonged.

Alas, the journey proved arduous. Many trials and tribulations beset the birds along the way. Some were overcome by a fierce dragon, others succumbed to despair over the length of the journey, while still others were led astray by the pleasurable wonders they beheld along the way. And some simply forgot the purpose of their destination.

Finally a small remnant of thirty birds reached the palace of the Simurg. Their hearts aflutter, they passed through the gates to the court-yard and through the courtyard into the chambers of the palace, where they wandered from room to room in search of the Simurg's throne.

At last they entered the innermost chamber, which, to their amaze-ment, was a hall of mirrors encircling an empty throne. As they gazed in confusion at their individual reflections, a great, unbearable longing filled their hearts. "O Simurg, where are you?" they cried out. At that moment their individual reflections merged in the image of one bird, and the Great Simurg appeared on the throne.

You see, *Simurg* means "thirty birds" in Persian. The Simurg is another name of the Shekinah, Herself the Bird of Golden Feathers, whose flight is the heartwing of our spirits and in whose reflection we become one. So it is written, "Each created being is a limb of the Shekinah."

4

Shekinah as the Longing for Wholeness

A KABBALISTIC PRAYER spoken before enacting a mitzvah says: "I perform this sacred deed for the sake of the unification of God and His Shekinah." This prayer expresses the longing deep in the soul of Jewish tradition for that which is broken to be repaired, for that which is lost to find its way home, and for the grace of Spirit to bring renewing love to wounded hearts.

Jewish tradition, as all religious traditions, tries to become a pathway toward inner and social harmony. Yet many of the paradigms meant to lead us toward that wholeness are based on sexist gender assumptions. The prayer just cited is an apt example. It refers to a common paradigm for wholeness: the marriage of the divine and the human. In this model of union, God is pictured as a king enthroned in the highest of heavens. His wife, the Shekinah, is exiled in the material world. The task of the male Jewish mystic is to arouse God's passion so He can copulate with the Shekinah and so send His seed/energy into the world.

In a time when so many women are trying to experience meaning in their life apart from their identification as wife, lover, or mother, we need metaphors other than sacred marriage to lead us toward a whole self. Even though many women enjoy marriage and children, many others (men as well) come from broken marriages, enjoy single status, have experienced sexual abuse, link their sense of accomplishment to their work, are not in heterosexual relationships, and do not image union with a male beloved as the ultimate goal.

Unfortunately, when women display authority outside the context of marriage, they are often demonized or isolated. Our earthly wisdom, creative intuition, lunar and cyclical knowledge, our erotic powers, and our ability to heal are viewed suspiciously at best and are denigrated and punished at worst.

As we begin to reconstitute these lost aspects of ourselves and redeem ourselves from our position as outcasts, we need spiritual paradigms and human role models, stories and historical memories that help us value our wisdom, our fearlessness, our sexuality, and our public works.

The search for stories that contain positive spiritual paradigms for women led me to the Near Eastern story about the descent of the Goddess Inanna to the underworld in quest of inner wisdom. The motif of the Goddess's search for a lost self speaks to contemporary women's quest for inner wisdom and an accurate representation of us in history. Rather than imaging ourselves completed by union with the opposite gender as the final destination, we look to Inanna to teach us how to use our courage and wisdom to heal ourselves so we can continue to grow into fullness.

I have a special tenderness for this story, since in a way it gave birth to the congregation I now serve. I told this story in 1982 on Rosh Hodesh Tevet, which is the new moon immediately after winter solstice. I told this story as a guided meditation into our personal depths. The women who were present became the core of twelve women who initiated the congregation and planned the first high holy days. Since that time I have come to appreciate the importance of this myth in the lives of women. I would like to restore the descent myth to its seasonal occasion, Rosh

Hodesh Tevet, so it can receive a day in the calendar year devoted to re-calling the prototype of all descent tales.

THE DESCENT OF INANNA

Inanna's descent into the underworld occurs in her later years, after she has attained her "bed" and "throne." She learns of the death of her sister Ereshkigal's husband and decides to pay a mourning call. Ereshkigal had been raped and carried off by her underworld husband many years be-fore. Now, at the time of his death, Inanna puts her ear to the ground, which is the Sumerian way of saying she seeks wisdom. Queen Inanna adorns herself with ceremonial jewelry and clothing and begins her per-ilous journey downward. She places her female ally Ninhursag at the point of her descent, instructing her to seek help in case she does not re-turn after three days.

As Inanna passes through each of seven gates on her way to the un-derworld, she is forced to shed one of her protective garments. Finally she arrives naked and alone before the stern gaze of her formidable sis-ter, Ereshkigal, queen of the underworld, who promptly fastens the eye of death on Inanna and hangs her corpse on a hook on the wall.

After three days Ninhursag obtains help from Inanna's father, Enki, who dispatches two tiny spirit-helpers to assist his daughter in her plight. The diminutive size of these two creatures allows them to pass through the seven gates undetected. When they enter the throne room, they find Ereshkigal groaning in the throes of labor. Ereshkigal cries out in pain, and they answer her and comfort her. Ereshkigal is delighted with their empathic response and offers them a gift of their choosing as a reward. They request the corpse of Inanna. Although the queen tries to dissuade them, she eventually grants their favor and releases Inanna to the upperworld, revived and renewed.[4]

THE DESCENT OF SHEKINAH

In Jewish storytelling traditions, the closest parallel to the descent of Inanna to her sister is the story of Jacob and Esau's night encounter in the river Yabakok as Jacob prepares to return home after dwelling in his

uncle's house for many years (Genesis 32:22–30). Like Inanna, he has acquired position and possessions. But before he can become Israel, he
must confront the brother he has tricked and neglected, Esau, just as
Inanna must stand before her neglected sister, Ereshkigal. Both seem
fearsome, both seek struggle unto death. But in the mysterious exchange
of life and death that the encounter produces, both Jacob and Inanna
emerge with new blessings and become their realized self, the self that
carries divine vision and the ability to heal. The struggle of the twins in
their mother's womb is repeated in their final struggle in the dark waters
of the night. But, unlike the first time, when Jacob was dragged into the
light by his brother, he must on his own accord secure light on his own
merit. Thus Jacob becomes Israel in his later years. But where is such a
story about women in Jewish tradition?

The possibility for a descent story lies in the fragmented tales of Shekinah, Lilith, and Eve. Although Lilith is usually associated with Jewish
legends, her story first appeared in cuneiform in 2300 B.C.E. in the
Inanna tale, where she represents an earlier aspect of Ereshkigal, the
wounded sister. When Inanna first plants her tree in the garden, Lilith, a
birdlike desert demon, sits in the crotch of the tree with her legs spread
wide. Distressed at the sight of Lilith, Inanna cries for her champion,
Gilgamesh, who banishes Lilith to the wasteland. Lilith flees when she
witnesses Gilgamesh slaying the serpent, who is her companion. Lilith
later appears in the Book of Isaiah (34:14) as a she-demon who abides in
the wasteland with her brother, Azazel, the goat demon.

In the kabbala, Lilith is the negative side of Shekinah. Unlike Shekinah, who tries to keep herself chaste, Lilith whores about, trying to seduce the holy men of Israel into sin. The foreign or slave woman has
been viewed since ancient times as a prototype for evil women, and
Lilith is also cast in this role. Her favorite activities are causing nocturnal
emissions, which the pious still consider a serious sin, and killing new-
born babies. Unlike the story of Jacob and Esau, where the twins are rec-
onciled and a blessing is created from their encounter, Lilith and
Shekinah never achieve such reconciliation. One is doomed to banishment, and the other sits on the footstool at the feet of her husband king.

Lilith and Shekinah remain polarized sides of the feminine persona and do not achieve integration or draw wisdom from their parallel existence. They never meet in the story. They are viewed as enemies rather than sisters.

But what happens if Shekinah assumes the role of Inanna? She is restored to her rightful throne. She is not in exile or seeking a mate. Instead she places her ear to the great below and hears her twin sister, Lilith, calling her from the depths. She dresses herself in the garments of her quest, all of which she must remove as she descends through the tree of life into the underworld. Alone and cold, she must ignite the fires in her own heart to face the fearsome and forgotten other. Imagine their encounter. What blessing will you receive from your subterranean sister?

I leave the rest of the story to you. You can use the story in guided meditation or as a theater exercise. Finish the story by asking yourself what Lilith can teach Shekinah, and what Shekinah can teach Lilith. In the descent tales, the rebirth of the forgotten sister/self happens through the medium of empathy. As we learn from the Torah, "Love your kin as you love yourself." Self-love is the gateway to loving the other. Jewish women are learning to love the abandoned and exiled elements of our soul. Those parts of ourself cast off by the patriarchal world are slowly becoming acceptable. We are assisted by our sisters and brothers, those brave men and women who do not fear this descent. They sense a new beginning.

As we collect to ourselves missing pieces of our psyche, we may stumble and even err in our choices. But we can never return to a myth that does not honor our most sacred quest, the quest to wholeness of being. Our descent to the underworld of our imagination will eventually allow us to give birth to a new vision of wholewoman for our own time.

5

Shekinah as the Call to Justice

By three things the world is preserved: by truth, justice, and peace.
If truth and justice are accomplished, peace will be in your gates.

Pirke Avot 1:18 (Sayings of the Fathers)

THE COMMAND to pursue justice is the heartbeat of Jewish teachings. "You shall not oppress a stranger; you know the heart of a stranger, for you were strangers in the land of Mitzryim" (Exodus 23:9). The ability to empathize with those who suffer motivates righteous action, especially in the treatment of those most marginalized and vulnerable in society. The Jewish social contract demands right treatment for those living at the edge as well as for those enjoying the privileged center.

As women press for social rights we need stories and prayers that can sustain and encourage our efforts. In the texts of Jewish tradition, women are portrayed as unable to effect their own redemption. Shekinah, the exiled element of the divine, is described as an outcast, a degraded woman, raped or abused, abandoned in her marriage, homeless in the streets, bereft of her children, and with none to comfort her. Shekinah is the consummate female victim.

When women are accredited with righteous actions in behalf of salvation, it is often related to their modesty or appropriate use of sexuality. The righteous women of the exodus generation, for instance, make themselves beautiful and tempt their husbands to lie with them in order to produce more children as a way of resisting Pharaoh's harsh decrees.

Yet Jewish women today need more stories that celebrate other aspects of our strength if we are going to ignite collective action in our own behalf.

As I sorted through Jewish sources, I found five feminine archetypes that display action and self-motivated energy in the service of women's redemption. These are midwife woman (*miyaledet*), prophet woman (*navia*), heart-courage woman (*eshet hayil*), lamenting woman and wise woman (*hachama*). These are the voices that call forth the people in righteousness and reveal the sacred visions that lead to peace in their own times. Along with these titles, I have suggested a corresponding ritual occasion to name the women who carry forth the tasks implied by their titles.

MIYALEDET: MIDWIFE WOMAN

Elohim was good to the midwives, and the people increased and became very numerous. Because the midwives loved AllSpirits, they were granted great houses/peoples of their own.

(Exodus 1:20–21)

The midwife woman works with her sisters. She is a spiritual and political healer who assists in the birth of freedom's child. She stands fearlessly before the highest secular and religious authorities and turns narrow beliefs about those who are viewed as expendable populations into pathways of liberation. Midwife woman revives the people's faith in their own birth-giving powers. She attends them, shares her wisdom of healing herbs, she teaches them how to name their children in ways that bless the Spirit of Life.

Shekinah is a midwife woman who sustains us through the pangs of labor, who opens our wombs and pushes forth new life. Shekinah helps us realize our common dream of justice. When women help women give birth to their dreams of freedom, and help one another in the struggle to make those dreams reality, Shekinah dwells in their midst.

During the ceremony of Rosh Hodesh Nisan, when we prepare ourselves for Passover, let us name the women of prophetic vision in our history, and let us name those who dwell among us now.

NAVIA: PROPHET WOMAN

> *Miriam the prophet, Aaron's sister, took the frame drum in her hand*
> *and all the women went out after her as Miriam led them in the*
> *response, "Sing to Adonai whose glory thunders. All the mighty*
> *warriors drown in the sea which gave us new life."*
> (Adapted from Exodus)

Navia the prophet woman gives voice to those voices silenced by oppression. She inspires the oppressed ones to use the tools of their culture to take back their power. Navia is poet, dancer, balladeer. With her gift for song, dance, and story she catalyzes the people to rejoice in their identity. Navia uses the drum. This is her tool. She plays the rhythms of beladi and causes women to rise up in song. She passes on the mantle of courage to stand before the multitudes and shout out freedom.

Shekinah is the voice of navia. She is the impulse to dance and drum, to speak the truth where deception covers our eyes. Navia speaks with the voice of Shekinah when she raises the ethical standards of the time and protests violence with acts of great kindness. When navia sings, Shekinah dwells in our midst.

The following is a song derived from Miriam's words in the Torah:

↭   *Miriam's Gifts*

Miriam drew her brother out of the river.

Miriam sang open the waters of the sea.

Miriam saw God as a midwife woman.

Miriam brought the desert her well of waters.

ESHET HAYIL: HEART-COURAGE WOMAN

What treasure [equals] a woman of courage?
Her value exceeds even rubies.
All the people place their trust in her.
(Adapted from Proverbs 31)

Eshet hayil, a heart-courage woman, walks with her head high, with bells on her ankles and a fearless heart. She is a spirit warrior. Her virtue is knowing when to coo like a dove and when to strike like a serpent. She is not afraid to tread new ground, to seek the wisdom of the underworld, or to wrestle the demons of her own soul. Eshet hayil knows the fruits of hard labor and discipline. She gives generously to family and friends yet does not exhaust the storehouse of her own spirit. When eshet hayil walks the spirit path, Shekinah walks with her.

Let us create occasions to invest our sisters, daughters, mothers, and grandmothers with the mantle of eshet hayil, thereby acknowledging their presence and accomplishments. We might wish, for instance, to honor a girl with the spiritual title of eshet hayil.

HACHAMA: LAMENTING WOMAN

The daughters of Jerusalem raise up lamentations,
They lift their voices and cry out.
My ways are scattered now,
But I remember when the women of Lydda
Would knead their bread,

Come up to Jerusalem to pray,
And return home before the bread leavened.
I remember when the women of Sepphoris would come to pray,
And still no one could gather figs earlier in the morning
Than those women.
I remember when the schoolmaster in Magdala
Used to arrange her candles, come to Jerusalem to pray,
And still arrive home in time to kindle them for Shabbat.
But my ways are scattered now, my paths are covered with thorns.
(Translated from *Ecca Rabbah*)

Lamenting woman weeps and rages at the madness of the times. She stands knee-deep in corpses, her hands blackened with the ashes of destruction. Through her lament she points a finger at those who unleash the horrors of violence upon the innocent. Her weeping is caustic; those smug in their privilege squirm in her truth. She demands nothing less than the return of her kin. She dresses in black and circles public places in her mourning. She holds up the pictures of the disappeared and forgotten. For them she weeps. And she will not cease her weeping until her children are returned to their place. When she weeps, Shekinah weeps with her.

✐ *The Lament of Shekinah*

When Shekinah saw Her daughter Jerusalem
Crying in the ashes of destruction
Shekinah began to weep.
Shekinah weeps and the angels cry with Her.
Shekinah weeps and the heavens and earth cry with Her.
Shekinah weeps and the mountains and valleys cry
    with Her.
Shekinah weeps and the people cry with Her.
Shekinah said, "As a reward for your weeping

I will restore the Beloved City
To her former joy."
       (Adapted from *Lamentations Rabbah*)

During the ceremonies of Rosh Hodesh Av, Tisha B'Av, or Yom HaShoa let us name the women whose power of mourning has helped release captives and challenged the rule of violence. Let us name those women in our history who have acted so and those who dwell among us now.

HACHAMA: WISE WOMAN

In former times if there was a conflict
They would come to Avel for counsel
And the matter would be settled.
I am one of the faithful of Yisrael
And you seek to destroy a city
And an Official Mother of Israel?
Why swallow up an inheritance of YHVH?
       (2 Samuel 20:18–19)

These are the words of the wise woman of the walled city of Avel, where people came to seek counsel and settle disputes. She is one of the wise women of her people. The hachama has gathered a storehouse of wisdom. She sits in counsel to young and old, to high and low. She mediates the middle way. Her words allow those in conflict to see the commonality of their interests. She points out waywardness without shaming those who err; she reduces pettiness in strife. Her humor is a softening agent to reduce the sting of hurtfulness and truth. When a hachama gives counsel, Shekinah dwells in her midst.

Let us name the wise elders who have counseled us in our history and in our lives. On the occasion of every holy day and life-cycle event, let us take time to name the wise women who have helped bring us to this day.

Shanu Hachamot

Shanu rabbanan is a Talmudic phrase that means "the sages taught." We will never know how often and to what degree the words of wise women informed the words of our male sages. I have changed the traditional phrase to *shanu hachamot*, which means "the wise women taught," so that we can begin to think of the elder women in our culture in that fashion. We learn from the Book of Proverbs that women stationed themselves at the crossroads, at city gates, and at the summit of mountains in order to impart their wisdom in public.

Let us continue to create public occasions to impart women's wisdom as well as to honor the learning we receive at our mothers' tables.

Wise Women Psalm

Shanu hachamot
Our elders taught us at the gate
Shekinah is present
When we sit and study Torah,
When we assemble in prayer,
When we teach our children to be kind.

Shanu hachamot
Our elders taught us at the crossroads
Shekinah is present
When we visit the sick,
Attend the dead to their graves,
Celebrate at weddings,
Receive guests into our homes,
Give assistance to the poor,
And care for the earth.

Shanu hachamot
Our elders taught us in the marketplaces
Shekinah walks with us
When we bring justice into the world.
They say: As Shekinah walks

So you shall walk, following in Her footsteps.
They say: Justice, justice you shall pursue.

Shanu hachamot
Our elders taught
Bloodshed, rape, and economic crimes
Cause the Shekinah to weep.
Lashon HaRah and bearing false witness
Cause the Shekinah to depart.
She does not dwell where She receives no welcome.

Shanu hachamot
Our elders taught
That to which you cleave will come to rest upon you.
One who cleaves to Shekinah,
Upon you will She rest.

Part Two

⮂ STORY

SHEKINAH COMING HOME

My desire to seek the Presence of God began in earnest when I learned about the Holocaust. I was fourteen. The shattering cry of Jews in Europe awoke my heart to the cries of all who suffer in the world, and I asked, Where is the God of justice?

Seven years later I flew home from Israel to be told at the airport that my mother had died. Her death cut my moorings. I drifted in rough waters, abandoned by my family of origin, who walked away from me. Where was the God who cares?

Luckily I was already committed to the path of becoming a rabbi, and I persisted in that endeavor. In my despair as an outcast daughter and in my new role as rabbinic student and rabbi, I continued to seek the Presence of God. But I could not find that Presence in the Father, Lord, King, Judge God of the traditional prayers. Kabbala helped me understand other roads toward feeling the Presence of God, but it was not enough. The God robed in kingly clothing could not heal my wounded heart.

Then I started to look in the most familiar place, in stories. My mother was a puppeteer and a teacher of creative dramatics for children. I always found comfort and strength in telling stories. That is why I was drawn toward the Jewish deaf community, which I served for eight years in New York City. As their rabbi I was in a privileged position to hear their stories and share their lives. They also deepened my understanding of the meaning of listening.

At the same moment, my Jewish sisters taught me to listen more carefully to women's stories. Women such as Liz Koltun, Judith Plaskow, Paula Hyman, and Sally Priesand were raising their voices in public places claiming that the relationship between men and women in Judaism was tipped in favor of the men, and that it had to change. In the freedom to pursue that insight, I found the feminine face of God, and she healed my soul. The Near Eastern myths of the goddesses Anat, Asherah, Inanna, Astarte, and Tiamat enchanted me. Threads that ran through their stories were woven into the fabric of the tales about Shekinah, Lilith, and many of the biblical ancestor tales. Their existence helped illuminate forgotten traditions. These forgotten traditions gave me a new place to stand on; they renewed my inner strength.

I am no longer an orphan. Shekinah feeds me at Her table. And I feel compelled to sing Her praises and tell Her many tales, to share recipes for living. Shekinah is the Presence that heals the world. She is the Mysterious Love in the heart of creation. Selah.

Torat HaShekinah
Ya,
She nodded,
Cupping my face in her leathery hands,
Your mothers took spiritnames
Often more than one
A hachama forsteyt fun eyn tsvey.

Now get in.
She brushed the hair away from my eyes.
I smiled and eased myself into the steamy waters
Of her wooden tub.
She sat by the edge and washed my hair in aloe,
Oiled my body with orange blossom and hibiscus
And hennaed my palms with intricate designs.
I stepped out and dried myself by the stove's red glow.
She watched me, my bubbe,
Then she removed her own shawl and placed it lovingly
    on my shoulders.
Sheyna, she whispered, iz gut.
The shawl enveloped me in golden threads
Primeval trees and magical beasts.
Tiny brass bells dangled on the fringe.
She began clapping as I swayed, the old one
Humming stories rooted in memory and earth,
tongue afire,
hips undulating,
chanting all the stories of my grandmothers
Hundreds of stories
given and passed on,
A chain of stories
Which I shall remember
And tell to my daughters and sons
Along with hers
In honor of Torat HaShekinah

6

Stories from the Mouths of Women

WINTER WINDS howled across Broadway. I cursed the cold Manhattan tundra and headed toward the McAlpin Hotel. As icy pellets blew into my face, I pictured my Polish great-grandparents, both orphaned by pogroms, trudging across the bleak winter landscapes of Europe in search of passage to better shores. I too was seeking better shores.

As I pushed through the revolving doors of the hotel, a rush of lobby air warmed my face. I unraveled my scarf and looked for the hall that would serve as the site of the first Jewish Feminist Conference, which was sponsored by the Jewish Feminist Organization in February 1973. Over three hundred Jewish women—from the most secular Bundists to the most extreme Orthodox—had come together to pose a question: Was Judaism sexist?

I remember feeling extremely uncomfortable in the presence of so many New York Jews. As a Reform Jew from a small town in Pennsylvania,

I felt intimidated by New York Jewish expertise. At the time I was not familiar with all the dos and don'ts of Orthodox practice, could not pray proficiently in Hebrew, and could not use Yiddish words like *maven, shmata,* or *oi gevalt* with any ease. Nonetheless I was thrilled to be part of a new community of Jewish feminists. We stood in the shadows of Jewish history with no male authorities present to evaluate the validity of our ideas as we talked Torah. For three days and nights we discussed, caucused, chatted, and prayed with a fervor equal to any yeshiva. I was astonished by the depth of knowledge so many women displayed. I realized that none of my Jewish teachers since high school had been women. Woman after woman ascended the platform to deliver her perspective on a wide range of topics, covering the role of Jewish women in history, ceremony, text, law, and community. I absorbed an astronomical amount of information during those days, but no one affected my grasp of the importance of the feminist perspective as an interpretive tool more than a diminutive professor of religion named Judith Plaskow.

Her head was barely visible above the dais, and her high-pitched, nasal voice was difficult to catch. But she told a story that became the seed of my feminist transformation. She told us of Lilith, the woman created before Eve. In those days, most of us had never heard of Lilith. If we had, it was as a baby killer and whore in the guise of a female demon. Judith introduced us to the *Aplabet of Ben Sirach,* an eighth-century C.E. text that contained the story of Lilith's creation. Born of night wind and fire (or in another version, born of mud and mire), the first woman, Lilith, claimed her autonomy from the start. She refused to assume the bottom position as Adam had commanded during their first sexual union. Lilith said: "I shall not lie below you, nor you lie above me, for we are both equal as we both come from the earth!" Then she ululated the Ineffable Name and fled the garden to the Red Sea. Abandoning God's paradise for one of her own making, Lilith acquired a lousy reputation in the patriarchal environment of Judaism, which portrays her as the ultimate uppity woman. She was demonized as an insatiable seductress and the queen of evil deeds.

Through the feminist eyes of Judith Plaskow, however, Lilith's act of so-called defiance against God and Adam was viewed positively as a demonstration of Lilith's freedom of spirit, a virtue that women struggling for freedom should learn to emulate. What Judith implied was the necessity to evaluate all the stories of Jewish tradition from a feminist perspective, since a feminist retelling of the tales could become a way to deconstruct sexism within Judaism. In order to do this, however, Judith needed to empower us to become tellers.

She did this by giving us a story of her own. Judith posed a question that was never asked by generations of male sages: Can you imagine what would happen if Lilith and Eve were to meet? In her tale, which she calls "Applesource," after Lilith flew the coop Adam requested a more malleable mate. He received Eve, a woman constructed from his own body. He warned his new wife not to get near the wall he built around the garden, because a horrible demonic creature lived on the other side. But Eve's curiosity led her to an encounter with this "forbidden fruit," her predecessor. Lilith greeted here kindly, and they began talking. "Who are you?" they asked each other. "What is your story?" They sat and spoke together of the past and then of the future. They talked for many hours, not once, but many times. They taught each other many things and told each other stories. They laughed and cried together until the bond of sisterhood grew between them.

Judith's rendition of Lilith caused me to begin my own investigation of women in the sacred narrative. If Lilith had somehow passed me by, how many other hidden fragments of women's lives were buried in the thousands of texts of my tradition? Torah is the heart and soul of Jewish narrative. What messages does it transmit about women?

FEMINIST DIRECTIONS IN STORYTELLING

Feminism allowed me to develop a set of questions by which I could examine a text. First it asked the question, What about the women? Who were they? How did they live? How are they being used by the text? How might they tell their own stories? Thus I came to reexamine all the women of the Bible, since they are featured in the stories we tell our children about our beginnings as a people. The biblical names familiar to us, Eve, Sarah, Rebecca, Rachel, and Leah, and the women in the Passover story, such as Miriam and the midwives, and the heroine Devorah, led me back to the primary source, the Torah.

I love Torah. The power of its narrative lies in its richness as a literary text. Yet, for me, Torah is both immensely satisfying and quite frustrating. The satisfaction comes from years of studying a text that never ceases to yield interpretive and imaginative fruits. Torah's greatness derives from its authority as a literary document whose presentation is like no other written work. Torah's style, poetry, and narrative, its tapestry of allusions and word play, its sweep of characters and events, its uncompromising starkness, its spectrum of genres, the anonymity of its authors, its ongoing relevance to Jewish people—all are elements of Torah's ability to continue to speak. My frustration with Torah comes from the restrictive social context of women in the text and from the ways the text has been used by subsequent generations to perpetuate the subordinate position of women in Judaism.

In the Torah women are mentioned most frequently in the context of their most honored function: to birth and protect favorite sons. On the one hand, we can grant that the Torah is a product of its setting and time. Patriarchy was the norm in all societies. Israelite women's lives were not substantially different from that of their neighbors. On the other hand, while the male heroes of the Bible lead lives of epic proportions, deal with complex issues over a lifetime, and are God's central protagonists in the drama of his involvement in Israelite history, women feature in supporting, never primary, roles. God almost never addresses them directly. Neither do we find stories about the birth and subsequent life of any female character nor the struggle of a mother to protect her daughter. With the brief yet precious exceptions of Miriam, Devorah, Hulda, Esther, the women in the Song of Songs, and the few wise women counselors, the Torah is not concerned with the stories of women apart from their motherly or wifely roles.

Today, however, the national mission of Jewish women does not require the basic paradigm of women using all means available to them to acquire sons. We no longer live merely vicariously, or receive fulfillment only through, the accomplishments of our children and husband. We need to express our creativity through other than domestic channels. How then are we to come to the central text of Jewish religion when the principal spiritual preoccupation of women is motherhood?

In fact Torah can be, as biblical scholar Phyllis Trible describes it, a text of terror. The rape of Dinah, for instance, can be a devastating story for women to read (Genesis 34:1–31). Her abduction by a man named Hamor (wild ass), son of Shechem, and subsequent rape is told from her brothers' and father's point of view. We never hear from Dinah, who has "gone out to seek the women of the land." All the commentaries about Dinah describe her rape as a kind of punishment for her wanton behavior, that is, going out by herself. The tale continues to serve as a kind of warning to women that the safest place is at home, away from "foreign women."

Yet, ironically, contemporary research into the treatment of women at home dislocates the patriarchal intent of the tale. Home is often, in fact, the place where women get raped. And if we are to construct a safe world for all women, we had best do so, not in isolation from one another, but by transgressing the usual racial and class boundaries.

The most difficult obstacle to a feminist interpretation of the Bible is simply the scarcity of texts about women. They are brought forward only as long as they serve their mostly procreative purposes, and therefore we know little about their lives. The story of Dinah, for instance, leaves us with only one intriguing phrase about her character: She went out to meet the women of the land. Sometimes we are left with only a title or a name. The only woman mentioned in the list of those who went down to Egypt with Jacob and his family is "Serach, the daughter of Asher." Who was she? The Torah does not tell us the reason for her mention in an otherwise male roll call. Devorah carries the title *Eshet Lapidot,* or "She who lights the fires." In her position as judge of Israel, what does this title imply about her tasks? The Torah is silent on this matter. Although silence in a story can be a place to fill in details with one's imagination, for women it is often a void into which our stories fall and become lost.

HONORING THE ORAL TRADITIONS
OF JEWISH WOMEN AS TORAH

Fortunately we are not the first generation of postbiblical Jews who need to give new meaning to the Torah, and our literary activities need not be limited to the Torah. From the Mishnaic period onward, Judaism has officially countenanced the view that an oral tradition, *Torah sheh b'al peh*, was given along with the written tradition of the Five Books of Moses at Mount Sinai. Moreover, the revelation of the oral tradition was seen as an ongoing process available to each generation. There has never been, even in the Torah itself, a single way of interpreting a story. We as a people have always recognized what is now called multivariant versions of a story, that stories by nature exist in multiple forms. We tell stories to illuminate the Mystery. Women's storytelling, however, has never been recognized as a sacred endeavor. Our storytelling has not been called Torah. But that does not mean we have been silent. Women do possess a tradition of storytelling in many forms, and it is time we honor that tradition as Torah.

One way to honor women's traditions of storytelling is simply to identify them as such, beginning with those from biblical times. Strewn throughout the texts of the Bible are women's poems, lamentations, wedding songs, temple psalms, oracular chants, war songs, eulogies, and festival liturgies, many of which are attributed to famous men. The Song of Songs, for instance, features many women's voices performing as wedding entertainers, a role they still play in the Middle East. Yet the entire collection is said to be authored by King Solomon. We know that Israelite women played in musical bands consisting of frame drums, flutes, and rattles. They performed dances exclusive to women called Maholot, and in that context delivered song-commentary about Israelite history. They were balladeers. Still, the tradition of women musicians and their role in Israelite society has only recently been a subject of scholarly appraisal by feminists, who teach us once again that we do have a history, one that has been largely ignored.

Another source of women's stories are the eighteen thousand collected tales in the Israeli Folk Archive in Haifa. They feature the voices of thousands of Jewish women from all over the world. Many of their stories relate alternative versions of the stories preserved in writing by men. Let me offer an example I heard from Dov Noy, the scholar who initiated the study of folklore as a legitimate academic enterprise in Israel. This particular story was first recorded by men in a tenth-century midrashic collection; women's versions of it have been collected by folklorists in the last fifty years in nine variant forms, all of which share the same ending.

The story is about twin sisters, one of whom commits adultery. She is discovered by her husband, who has the right under the biblical adultery law known as *sotah* to force his wife to undergo the ordeal of bitter waters to prove innocence or guilt. She must drink water mixed with the ashes of a paper inscribed with the name of God. If she is innocent, she lives. If she is guilty, she drowns in the liquid, which magically expands inside her.

In the tenth-century midrash the guilty woman begs her identical twin sister to take her place in the ordeal. Her sister, who has never transgressed, agrees. Conspiring together, they fool the suspicious husband and the priest and pass the test. Overjoyed at their victory, the sisters kiss each other on the lips. But a drop of the deadly water lingers on the lips of the innocent twin, and her sister is exposed to the deadly water and dies.

In the women's oral versions, however, the twin who passes the test returns home to the guilty sister, who says, "Now I am free again to do what I like." Her twin admonishes her, saying, "Everyone might stray once, but do not repeat the same mistake a second time." The guilty sister agrees and learns her lesson, and life continues for both of them.

If we did not possess women's oral versions of the story, we would have no idea that this story was told differently by women than by men.

"Tell me a story from your mouth, Mama." That is how my son, Nataniel, requests stories from the oral tradition. Stories from the mouth are powerful because they come from an intimate place in the teller to instruct and entertain the listener. In the kabbala, the Shekinah is identified with the oral tradition. She is the talking mouth, the word illuminated in living speech, the story that blossoms like fruit from the tree of life. Shekinah is the hidden root of stories. The Torah itself speaks of *Torat emecha,* "the Torah of your mother." Life instructions are transmitted through storytelling, and women have always engaged in this art. In our biblical role as *Em Yisrael,* Mother of Israel, we serve the people as interpreters of God's voice. Elder women such as Sonya the Hachama (Sonya the wise), whose picture appears in Beatrice Weinrib's book *Yiddish Folktales,* sat around shtetl stoves with all the generations gathered round to delight and instruct all present.

The existence of variant endings to stories gives modern interpreters and storytellers permission to revise tales that denigrate women. This is not to say all women are one-dimensional heroines with feminist perspectives. Our lives are vastly different. But we nonetheless need to revision the tales that are meant to instruct and give meaning to our lives.

A feminist approach to the Torah begins with the question, How might women have told their stories if they were central, rather than peripheral, characters in the Bible? What happens when we let Dinah speak in first person about her rape? When Miriam becomes the prophet who leads us through the parting seas? When we transform Rachel and Leah's stories into a tale about two loving sisters instead of jealous rivals? When we allow biblical women a story beyond their roles as mother? Stories are the medium through which women learn about each other and widen the circle of shared experience. Through storytelling we add to the wisdom contained in the traditional sources and help one another envision a future in which men and women have equal opportunities to tell stories in public.

I would like to refer to Torah from the perspectives of women as *Torat HaShekinah.* Torat HaShekinah recovers and invents a sacred narrative that is about the lives of women. So may it come to be.

The stories in *She Who Dwells Within* retell biblical tales from creation through the exodus generation. Aside from Queen Esther and Devorah, the women of Genesis and Exodus are the best known. They also present the greatest challenge, since most of them are bound up in the role of mother. I have divided these stories into three categories.

"Primeval Ancestors" explores the mythical women of beginning times (Tehom, Shekinah, Lilith, and Eve); "Tribal Mothers" retells the stories of the first mothers of the people Israel: Sarah, Hagar, Rebecca, Rachel, and Leah. "The Freedom Generation" celebrates the six women associated with the story of Passover.

In retelling these stories I have drawn on many sources, in addition to the text itself, including Goddess mythology from the Near East; midrash or classical Jewish legends; Jewish folktales, fairy tales, songs, and proverbs told by women, and the stories I hear from women living today. It is so important for us to tell our stories, as the following incident illustrates.

Snow is the winter garment of Shekinah. And we were snowed in. Twenty women traveled to Rowe Retreat Center in western Massachusetts to study Jewish feminism and mysticism only to be told that a fierce snowstorm was headed our way that evening. After much discussion, all but two women stayed. The weekend was magical. We marched and sloshed our way back and forth from the dining hall to the barn to the sauna through snow piled three feet high. We sang and laughed.

I planned one session to uncover an important passage in their life for which there had been no ceremony or public acknowledgment. After a guided meditation, we passed a talking stick to share our stories. Many women were crying as they mourned the lost occasions and the absence of recognition. In the telling, however, there was healing, as long-held secrets were revealed. An older woman told her daughter, who was present, that she had nursed her at the breast, but this was viewed with such horror by her family that she kept it a secret all these years. Now, in the welcoming company of these women, she told her story.

As a follow-up to recounting these passages, the women divided into groups according to common themes and created prayers for those lost times. The prayers were spoken, and more stories were told. In that weekend of telling, the Shekinah who resides in our hearts found a resting place in our stories.

We all have stories to tell. Our culture's survival and richness rest on the power of storytellers. Storytellers transform dogma into joyful noise!

Too often, however, we surrender our words to authorities. Rabbis give weekly sermons, lecturers exhort from the bimah, expert panelists argue and debate; but seldom, if ever, does the synagogue facilitate storytelling by the members of the community. If Judaism is successful at becoming nonsexist, then the synagogues and classrooms, the yeshivas and seminaries, the holy days and special occasions will reverberate with the voices of women and men telling stories.

7

Primeval Ancestors

> *The mothers say*
> *by a name*
> *we know when spirit touched the heart*
> *and turned a life around.*
> *The mothers say*
> *Shekinah dwells in that name.*
> *The mothers say*
> *when we stray*
> *or become lost*
> *our names call us back.*
> *Blessed be Shekinah*
> *who bestows Her spirit upon us*
> *and awakens our true names.*

    GENEALOGIES CREATE family ties and a sense of be-
longing. Whenever I conduct a ceremony with women, I
ask participants to name themselves by their Jewish name
and then to list their mothers and grandmothers on their mother's side
as far back as they can go. Like so: I am Miriam, daughter of Tzvia (she
did not know her Hebrew name but went by Harriet), daughter of
Bessie, daughter of Delia, daughter of Jennie from Philadelphia, daughter of Henrietta from Hesse Castle, Austria.

This simple ritual of naming often brings women to tears. For many it
is the first time in their lives they are asked to provide a genealogy
through the line of their mothers. The women in our families are seldom honored in a formal way. "To remember" and "to be male" come
from the same Hebrew root, *Z-Ch-R*, because family identity is passed
on by telling stories about the men. To remember by naming connects
us to our place of origins and grounds us in the place we came from. In
so doing we begin to understand and to navigate the present. We therefore turn to our origins as recorded in the Torah.

Jewish women need a genealogy that restores our mothers' names to
the sacred history of our people. But the Torah does not contain ge-
nealogies of women. Nor does it interpret the meaning of women's
names. Yet, as Geoffrey Hartman, a professor of English and compara-
tive literature at Yale University, points out, "Each story's reasoning
upon a name, recharges the name . . . nomen becomes numen (name
becomes spirit) through the story inspired by it."[5] If we are to create inspired stories, we need to remember the meaning of our mothers'
names.

A ceremonial way to recharge our mothers' names is by singing the
Mother Chant, a genealogy I wrote to be chanted and danced by women
before reading from the Torah or at women's ritual occasions. Each
name is translated by an English phrase that suggests the nature of
Shekinah's challenge and blessing in their lives. It begins not with Eve
but with Shekinah's ancestor, Tehom, the Near Eastern Goddess of creation, and so acknowledges the first name of God.

By representing each of the names as a dance movement, we can model the tradition of women's performance at sacred occasions recorded in the Bible and practiced by women from Sephardic and Middle Eastern Jewish communities to this day. I invite you to create your own melodies and movements in the presentation of Mother Chant. I also invite you to create your own genealogy of names to be sung in honor of your family of origin.

WOMEN'S GENEALOGY FROM TORAH

Mother Chant

Brucha Ya Shekinah hanotenet orah l'sapair sipurim.
Blessed are you who gives your light
To inspire the telling of sacred tales.
Night Sea Woman   Tehom
Light That Dwells Within Woman   Shekinah
Fiery Night Woman   Lilith
Let There Be Life Woman   Hava
Mother of the Tent Women   Adah
Flute Song Woman   Zilah
Voice of the Flood Woman   Na-amah
See Far Woman   Sarah
Outcast Woman   Hagar
Pillar of Salt Woman   Eshet Lot
Praises All Life Woman   Yehudit
Earth Smelling Sweet Woman   Basmat
Buffalo Woman   Rivkeh
Talking Bee Woman   Devorah
Soft Eyes Woman   Leah

Soft Heart Woman   Rachel

Truth Seeking Woman   Dinah

Desert Eagle Woman   Asnat

Smells of Time Woman   Serach

Horn of Freedom Woman   Shifra

Helping Hand Woman   Puah

Golden Cloud Woman   Yocheved

And never was there a prophet like Miriam HaNavia:

She sang open the waters of the sea,

And all the people passed through to freedom.

T'halelli yah t'halleli ya t'halleli ya t'halleli ya

la la la la la la la la la la la la laa!

NIGHT SEA WOMAN, TEHOM

Tehom is the first name recited in the Mother Chant. In the Bible Tehom is the watery abyss, the primal sea. The spiritwind of Elohim hovers over Tehom in the moment before the creation of light. In her most ancient guise, however, Tehom is the Creator, sometimes imaged as a great water serpent with wings. I have found the image of the Creator as Serpent Woman in Chinese and Native stories of the Americas as well.

The Tehom of the Bible is based on the Babylonian Mother of the gods, Tiamat, who is mentioned in the Babylonian creation story called *Enuma Elish.*

Just as Elohim is a noun with a plural ending but is spoken of as a singular being, so Tiamat has a plural ending but is spoken of as a singular being, the Mother of all the gods. In the Bible, however, the forces of nature are no longer portrayed as divine beings. They have been transformed into natural forces created by Allspirits Elohim. The Israelites deeply respected nature and saw Elohim's majesty reflected in the natural world. But they traded polytheism for monotheism, and they suppressed the belief in a Mother Goddess in favor of a male god.

The suppression of goddesses is also evident in the literature of Baby-lon some one thousand years prior to the rise of the Israelite nation. In the *Enuma Elish,* Tiamat has already undergone the limitation of her powers. Although she is mentioned in the creation tale as the Mother of all, her acts of creation are not described as they were in the Sumerian tales that preceded the *Enuma Elish.* By that time, "many of the former functions of the goddesses had been taken over by the gods."[6]

In the *Enuma Elish,* Tiamat represents the old order of the gods. She and her husband are challenged by the younger generation. At first she refuses the challenge, but after the murder of her husband, Tiamat is forced into battle against her grandson Marduk. Marduk slays his grand-mother by slicing her in half. He then assumes the leadership of the pan-theon of the gods. Marduk imposes a new order in which male gods are the chief authorities and the goddesses fall under their dominion.

The story of Tehom reminds us that women's fall from grace came not with the eating of forbidden fruit but through their suppression.

The archetype of Mother Creator is nonetheless ever present in our psyches. I call on the name and story of Tehom to remember the abiding sea of our memories, a sea so deep and so wide that it contains every-thing that ever happened to women.

An appropriate ceremonial occasion for the recitation of Tiamat/ Tehom poems, prayers, and stories may be the second day of Rosh HaShanah. As the stars emerge, sit around a fire or enter the shvitz and tell the old creation stories as a way to renew our own powers of cre-ation for the coming year.

Tehom Prayer for the Second Day of the New Year

Tehom
Night Sea Woman
Salt and crystalline
Life arose in the rapture
Of your briny green.

Tehom

Black Hole Woman

The mystery of your pulling inward

Our minds cannot follow.

All logic and learning disappear

In the immenseness of your hollow.

The prayer that follows can be recited by midwives and friends around a woman in labor. Using a rattle to create a rhythm can help the birthing woman's breathing.

✤ Tehom Prayer for Giving Birth

Tehom

Inward chasm

Womb Grave Desire

Rising with desire

She births light into song,

   Song into light,

All moving

All twirling

   All spinning

   All whirling

Tehom births

Souls

Colors

Rhythms

Flesh

A chorus of angels

A glorious throne

A tree of life
and moon
earth
earth
Tehom births
rippling
spreading
  spiraling
  weaving
She births.

Tiamat's Demise

There is a time to be born and a time to die, and even in the midst of death, to reemerge, to influence the living. So stories about the Mother of the gods persist. It is her very endurance that gives women faith and hope in their ability to transform and give new life to the struggle for freedom.

Tehom's Blood

Her belly bloated from the storm
She swallowed into herself
Tehom moaned,
Unable to vent her terrible rage
Or to dispatch the fearsome legions to the kill.
He simply sliced her up
Like the butchering of an old cow
Left her carcass to the flies
Her blood to fertilize the fields
Her dismembered bones to the desert floor.

So complete in his victory over her
He failed to notice the underworld
Growing beneath his feet.

Red Sky Woman, Red Earth Woman,
Your own son
Crushed your skull with an ax,
Let the wind carry off your blood.
Your blood is the river that flows inside us
And we walk upon you.
Your children walk upon you,
Grandmother of Creation.

The Jewish day begins at sunset with the coming of the night. It echoes the story of creation in Genesis: darkness comes before light. In the following prayer I have replaced the name of God usually associated with this prayer, YHVH Tzevaot, with Tehom Tzevaot. The word *Tzevaot* conjures up a vast array, or an army, of stars. In this prayer I return to the original image of Tehom as the dark womb of the cosmos itself.

⟜ *Prayer for Maariv in the Woods*

Doors like ships sail open
The rush of children to the wood
And we, lured by forest green,
Descend into twilight,
Disrobe by a forest spring.
Climbing down a mossy stair
We discern Her fires burning there
And settle in.
A grace of evening breath

Cools the air and brings to life
The cacophony of forest at the edge of night,
The rising song of toad and frog
Wolf and cat, owl and bat.
Set between the dancing leaves
And the quiet of the trees
We receive the shadows of the night
And expand our horizons with her starry light.
Ya Tzevaot Tehom
Rolling back day
Spinning forth night
Light to dark to light
Swirls the glorious cosmic array.
Starry Night Woman,
This too is your name

LIGHT THAT DWELLS WITHIN WOMAN, SHEKINAH

Although Shekinah does not appear in the Bible, and does not become the feminine Presence until the first millennium C.E., she nonetheless carries images and stories associated with the ancient goddesses of the Near East. "Under the wings of the Shekinah" is a phrase in Jewish prayers that portrays the Shekinah as a bird protecting the children in her nest. She is sometimes an eagle and sometimes a dove. Asherah, the Sea Goddess, Mother of the gods of the Canaanite and Phoenician peoples, was also called a dove. Shekinah as Birdwoman emerges from the ancient iconographic form of the goddess as the Water Serpent with wings.

Birdwoman Shekinah is the magical spirit of life arising from the abyss with breath and light. Women dream of flying, of soaring over the conventions and ideological formulations that clip our wings. Shekinah is our authentic self, our internal birdwoman. She is the spirit of the eagle who transcends the constrictions of oppression and flies into the free, open spaces of the wilderness. Women need Shekinah's wings.

We also need images of her fierceness, her uncompromising nature when it comes to defending things sacred to her. Shekinah for me is the Primeval Dragon, unfurling her long, coiled tail to reveal the cosmic egg. Her fiery breath, wide and jagged wings, prismatic skin, and wise old eyes summon me into the wildness of my own creative spirit. Here then is my version of Genesis 1:

The Primeval Dragon Creates

In a time before time
That nobody knows,
Before sky stretched out
And earth arose,
She was there thinking,
All coiled up.
She thought,
I'll unfold
My serpentine self,
Unfurl my snaky wings
And fly off somewhere
I deem it wise.
So she did just that,
Cast her shadow on MamaDeep
Like a dove over the watery heap
Beating her wings
She stirred things up.
Is that how it all began?
Her laying an egg
And letting it sink in?

FIERY NIGHT WOMAN, LILITH

Tehom and Shekinah are names for the Mystery of creation in her feminine attire. Lilith and Eve, by contrast, are more human than divine. Nonetheless they both emerged from the mythology of the ancient goddesses of the Near East. In Jewish legends told by men, Lilith uses her erotic powers to subvert male control. The recent popularity of Lilith's story among feminists also has to do with her uncontrollable and self-determined nature. But many women possess an ambivalent relationship to their power. Lilith is the shadowy side of our power, the power that has not yet been tamed and put to use in the service of our greatest personal gifts, whatever they may be. Lilith is a side of feminine power with which we must reckon. When she is repressed or dominated, she becomes desperate, enraged, and insane. When she is acknowledged and loved for her fire, she becomes a source for positive creation. Tracking our Lilith nature is the key to our spiritual awakening.

The first time I composed a story for Lilith (in 1973), I was feeling angry about the loss of women's history. I created a performance that dealt with these feelings. Lilith has been a performance piece for me since the beginning of my storytelling as a rabbi, more than twenty years ago. I recall with fondness working in the mid-1970s with Dafna Soltis, a dancer and actress who brought Lilith to life in the following story through the beauty of her movement and the freedom of her spirit. I especially remember a time we performed this piece in a conservative Jewish community in Colorado Springs. The following day we hiked in the Rockies. In an isolated wood she shed her clothing, and I timidly followed suit. The next hour was liberating, a gift of Lilith's untamed spirit.

Lilith-Eve
First Tale, 1973

In the beginning
God made the earth and the sky and the sea.
God reached into the waters,
formed a womb in her hand,
and put it in the sky.

Then
with her own breath
God filled the womb with Lilith,
first woman.
Deep inside the womb
Lilith began her birthing.
The womb grew heavy with woman
until one day Lilith pushed her arms outward,
tore the walls which held her,
to reach the sky.
The sky, smiling, received her.
Lilith embraced all life
with her wings of fire
not knowing where sky began
and her own self ended.
Lilith looked down,
saw a shadow on the waters.
She saw herself hovering over the deep.
Lilith rejoiced.
Thinking she had found another like herself,
she spoke to the reflection
which did not answer.
First loneliness.
And God said: It is not good
for woman to be alone.
I will make her a companion.
As Lilith is sky
so man shall be earth.

And God made man
from the dust of the ground,
breathed into him the breath of life,
and man became a living being.
Then God brought Lilith to dry land.
There upon the soil
Lilith became still,
seeing a place which did not move
like wind or water.
Lilith said:
I will stay a while.
Then he appeared and came toward her.
His eyes still spoke of birth, like hers,
yet she knew a difference.
This one stood solid on the ground.
He said: I am Adam child of Adamah.
Walk with me and I will show you the earth.
Lilith smiled and said: I am Lilith
with wings of fire.
Come and I will show you the sky.
But Adam, afraid of Lilith's wings of fire,
fell to the earth.
Lilith, needing her companion,
removed her wings of fire,
hurled them to the sky.
Adam saw Lilith without her fire.
No longer afraid,
he rose to meet her.

Woman and man walked together
sharing memories of their own first hours.
Lilith remembered a spirit on the waters,
called to the sun to return her fire.
But Adam, still afraid of woman's fire,
forced Lilith to the ground,
hoping to make her more like himself.
But she continued calling.
Then Adam understood
the power of his holding
forced himself down upon her.
Lilith felt his strength as pain,
closed her eyes,
first sleep of terror.
Deep inside her own darkness
under the fear of man
Lilith forgot her sky birth
and awoke without memory.
Eve,
second woman.
Eve opened her eyes,
saw Adam standing large before her.
He moved and revealed the sun.
Adam said: I will call you woman
because you come from man.
Serve me
and I will protect you from strange fires.
Eve upon the earth

gave herself to man.
And God, sad parent of creation,
wept seeing woman slave to man
and man afraid of woman.
God knew she must give them life and death,
the passing of generations,
so one future man and woman
could come together
as intended at creation.
And God planted the tree of knowledge in the garden,
   saying
You must choose eternity or knowledge
for on the day you eat this fruit
you shall surely die.
And Eve said: I want to know
and felt a strange remembering.
She saw the tree was good for food
and a delight to the eyes
so she took the fruit and ate it
Adam ate with her.
Then Eve heard the evening wind
moving in the garden
and some dark memory stirred her soul—
a memory of fire,
a spirit on the waters.
Adam saw death,
the lost eternity of man
and said: In pain you shall bear my children;

your desire will be toward me.
Eve left the garden with her master
mourning a self not quite remembered.
Lilith,
we are your children,
we are the changing generations.
Help us recover our wings of fire
so we can come together
woman and man
as intended by God
in the beginning of creation.

The Lilith I created in 1973 has been replaced in performance with a bawdy version of the original tale. But the story of Lilith has not yet arrived at a final stage for me, and I guess it never will. Lilith keeps manifesting and revealing new aspects of her nature. The most recent is her proclivity for dirty stories that almost never involve romance. She says the words *penis* and *vagina* in public just to see who blushes. Are you blushing?

LET THERE BE LIFE WOMAN, HAVA

Hava, or Eve, is the last in the cycle of primeval ancestor tales and belongs to the collection of stories about the first woman that appear worldwide. Eve is probably the most commented upon woman in the world, but it is hard to find anything positive said about her in Jewish sources, other than midrash that describes her marriage to Adam.

It is only by reading the creation stories of other peoples that we can identify elements of her power neglected by Jewish tradition. Many of the symbols and stories associated with the goddesses of the ancient Near East, such as serpents, the tree of life, the quest for knowledge, and the glory of female sexuality, are recast in negative terms in the story of

Eve. Instead of planting the tree of life in her own garden, like Inanna did, Eve is forbidden to eat from its fruit altogether lest she become too much like God. Instead of being a sign of her oracular wisdom, the serpent tricks Eve. Unlike Inanna, Eve does not descend to the underworld and is punished for her curiosity. And Eve's sexuality becomes a burden and a curse to her, "for her desire is unto her husband," and she must labor painfully in childbirth. Finally Eve, unlike Inanna, is ashamed of her body. There are no songs to her vulva like those Inanna sings. Yet the old associations persist in the tale, and women have begun to retrieve them and weave them back into the story as positive elements in the life of Eve.

One of the most exciting pieces of lost information recently rediscovered is the archaeological evidence of women's contribution to the formation of human culture. In many cultures of the ancient Near East, women are credited with the invention of pottery, agriculture, bread baking, writing, weaving, dream interpretation, the oracular arts, the art of lamentation, and the art of healing with herbs. Yet in the Bible men are given credit for the invention of culture, except for law and sacred rituals, which are attributed to God. Jewish origin tales need to reflect women's true gifts to human development and to the people Israel. The Eve I have imagined in my re-creation reasserts women's inventiveness and ingenuity.

I have translated Hava's name as "Let There Be Life Woman" in order to honor her creativity and resourcefulness. I see Hava as Everywoman, constantly growing and integrating new experiences into her storehouse of wisdom. She eats from the tree of knowledge not once but many times as she expands the horizons of her understanding.

By seeing Hava as a woman who pursues knowledge by making choices and taking risks, we erase the taint of sinfulness that has attached itself to her persona. Some scholars contend that the story of Adam and Eve presents woman in a positive light because of the term *ezer c'negdo,* "helpmate," but the wordplay used to tell the story does not support this view. Hava is drawn from Adam's rib or side, which is *tzela* in Hebrew. Yet this word also means "to limp." The intended pun suggests that men are wounded and limping from their contact with women, a meaning that is reinforced by the role the text gives to Hava as the one who coaxed Adam to eat the forbidden fruit, thereby resulting in his banishment from the garden of delights. Hava is a dubious helpmate to Adam and reflects the ambivalent feelings men have about women.

By transforming Hava into Everywoman, we also transform Adam into Everyman. Adam must also seek wisdom, taste death, leave the garden of his youth, and make his way in the world. By changing the way we tell the story, we can help men and women foster a sense of mutual struggle toward authenticity without the need for notions of inferiority or superiority on either side. By asking ourselves how we might retell the story so it reflects our struggle for mutuality and respect, we have already initiated necessary changes in the way we see each other.

The cycle of Everywoman Eve is meant for telling when we read the story of Genesis during Simchat Torah. I have borrowed traditional midrash and refashioned the tales. One midrash describes Adam and Eve as an androgynous creature that was separated by God, and another negatively assesses all the parts of Eve's body. We find some stories about Eve's inventiveness in the apocryphal *Books of Adam and Eve,* and I have drawn on them as sources for an Eve who invents many things. Another stream in Eve's story relates her to the tripartite image of the Goddess as maiden, mother, and crone. Many Jewish legends describe Hava's birth, her quest for knowledge, her experience of motherhood, and her death.

✧ *Awakening*

Shekinah gazed upon the sleeping form of HeShe.
"I shall divide this being
So HeShe can find loving companionship
Like the other creatures in the garden."
HeShe lay asleep in the grass
Curled up like a snake in the warm sun

Dreaming of angels.
Shekinah thought,
"Which part of the body
Shall I take to form the woman?
Perhaps from the mouth
So she can tell stories like Serach,
The woman who smells of time.
Perhaps the eyes
So she sees the inside truth of things
Like Soft Eyes Woman Leah.
Perhaps from the neck
So she walks with pride
Like the daughters of Zelophehad
Who are Mahlah, Noah, Hoglah, Milcah, and Tirzah.
Perhaps the ears
So she hears my laughter
Like See Far Woman Sarah.
Perhaps the heart
So she flows with tender mercies
Like Soft Hearted Woman Rachel.
Perhaps the arms
So she heals and restores with touch
Like the Hebrew midwife women.
Perhaps the legs
So she goes out seeking wisdom
Like Truth Seeking Woman Dinah.
Perhaps from the flower of her passion
So she enjoys the fruits of her body

Like Shulamit."
Then Shekinah blessed every part of woman's body,
*   saying,*
"Be pure of heart
and always know you are created in My image."
Then she awoke, first woman.

The onset of menstruation is not mythologized in Jewish sources. I
have created this moment in Eve's life and connected it to the covenant
of Rosh Hodesh. It is adapted from Talmud Saferin.

⇔ *First Blood*

In the darkest cycle of the moon
Hava watched her body change.
She found a quiet place among the trees to brood.
Suddenly her body swelled
And released first blood
Which mingled with the earth's dark soil,
Reddening the ground.
Adamah she called the earth, red like me.
Then a doe appeared
And told her the secrets of the flow,
Held up the mirror of generations.
Hava sighed.
After three days
The blood ceased to flow.
She went down to the river
And marked the first passage of her womanhood.
She sang:

Night sky

moon moon

grows full and wise

moon moon

thins in the dark

moon moon

tallit ha-mavet

moon moon

sliver of light

moon moon

soul of the skies

moon moon

we lift up our eyes

moon moon

stand straight with a dance

moon moon

circle around

moon moon

chanting the hum

Brucha Yotzri-ich

Brucha Koni-ich

Brucha Bori-ich

Keep evil away

moon moon

braid us a crown

moon moon

shalom shalom shalom

amen amen

selah

hallelujah!

Hava, the first mother, also witnessed the first fratricide. This moment is recorded in the midrash to explain why Hava called her second child Hevel, meaning "in vain." In this fragment Hava sees in a dream what is to befall her children. In the midrash Hava is said to have given birth to twins, a sister for Kayin and a sister for Hevel. Did these sisters survive? Did they lament the death of their brother? How did they comfort their mother, and each other? These tales remain to be told.

⤳ *Mother Eve*

My body changed
a great mound of child in my body
Adam saw
and touched the dance

In the summer as the child pushed out,
my belly touched the earth.
Like a fire forging metal into plow
I brought this child out
and named him Kayin.

With the second child
I faced the rising sun
and saw the blood of this unborn
fill the mouth of his brother.
Kayin drank without pity
but the blood would not stay down;
it spilled out of his mouth to the ground,
but the ground shrieked and hurled his blood to the tree;

the tree cried and hurled his blood to the stones;
the stones screamed and hurled his blood to the air,
where it remained flying about endlessly.

I wept
how I wept.
I saw my own child murder his brother
so I called this child Hevel

Hava is also known in Judaism as woman of the plants, preserving the ancient association of women with the healing arts. Healers do not cure only the flesh. A person's sickness affects her total being and her relationship with the divine. This is adapted from the *Books of Adam and Eve* in the Apocrypha.

OLD WOMAN EVE

Hava ate from the tree of knowledge because she saw that the tree was good to behold, good to eat, and good to make one wise. She ate from the fruit and gave all the animals of the garden as well. When Snake bit into the fruit, she said, "Hava, I bless you with the power to create and destroy worlds just as Shekinah creates and destroys worlds. Just as Shekinah brings death and revives, so you will have the power to bring death and revive."

"How can it be?" asked Hava.

Snake showed her how to shed old skins. When Hava ate from the tree of life, all the trees of the garden lost their leaves except for the fig in the center of the garden. Hava heard the sound of the shofar trumpeting through the garden and knew it was the voice of Shekinah.

Hava said, "I was naked in the world, and I knew the day of discernment had come upon me."

Hava set out and learned to follow the four directions of the river that flowed from the midst of the garden. She wrapped herself in a garment from the skin Snake had given her. She formed an earthen vessel from the soil. Using fire she obtained from the whirling swords that guarded the entrance of the garden, she built a hearth. Hava planted the seeds she collected from the grasses in the garden and harvested grain. She ground the grain into meal and served her family flat cakes in honor of the gifts of creation.

In her later years, Hava was known as a woman of knowledge among her people. She could return to the original garden and bring back healing oils from the root of the tree of life. Hava watched the stars and the moon in the sky. Her own body and the movement of the heavens let her know when to plant and when to harvest, when to gather and when to move on.

When it came time to die, Hava gathered her people around her and said: "I take up the earth. Earth speaks as my witness. I carve my life on a tablet of stone. A cradle of light carried on the wings of eagle. Holy beings ride on the flow. Sweet smoke is in the wind. I take up the earth and surrender my soul." Then Hava lay in the womb of the earth and died. They rubbed her body with Adamah's blood, the red soil of her birth, and covered her and mourned many days.

8
Tribal Mothers

THE GOD OF Abraham, Isaac, and Jacob was also the God of Sarah, Rebecca, Rachel, and Leah. The mothers (*emahot* in Hebrew) are also our tribal elders. They are the old ones whose stories are told at sacred occasions. They exist in the folktales of Jews around the world. A righteous woman in Poland is visited by four women in the mikveh, who she later realizes are none other than the mothers. A woman in Tunisia gives birth in her later years and sees Sarah in a dream blessing her. The names of Sarah, Rebecca, Rachel, and Leah are invoked in the private and public prayers of Jewish women that they utter before lighting the Sabbath candles, while they attend a birth, before taking a mikveh, or at a weaning ceremony.

The stories of the four mothers are told and retold in the annals of the Talmud and midrash, in Sephardic folk ballads and Yiddish poetry. Like Elijah, they return to women to confer advice and offer blessings. Sarah blesses us with the power to bear fruit from withered ground. Rebecca blesses us with the cleverness and persistence of coyote, Leah blesses us with the wisdom to draw love from the earth, and Rachel blesses us with the courage to take what is ours and to raise up a loud voice for all who suffer. Because Sarah, Rebecca, Rachel, and Leah are ancestor spirits, we draw on the light that radiated from their lives.

Although women seek to give meaning to their lives beyond their role as mothers, mothering is still a central aspect of our identity. Raising and tending to children, life projects, friendships, and all that lives with us every day belongs to the domain of motherhood. Mothers feed and nurture even as they let go of and surrender to the people and projects they raise. The sacred way of mother is a balance between limitless loving and necessary boundaries. Sarah, Rebecca, Rachel, and Leah can teach us wisdom as we practice the art of mothering. By honoring these mothers as full partners in the early stories of our people, we honor mothers in our own time as well.

SARAH AND HAGAR

Sarah and Hagar are the first matriarchs of the Jewish and Muslim peoples. Unfortunately these two female characters are set in the context of the barren woman motif, which portrays women's struggle for sons and reproductive blessings in a society concerned with male inheritance.

It is extremely important for women to acknowledge the literary nature of the text and to begin to understand the part these characters play in the story. The entire Abrahamic cycle is designed to highlight Abraham's life, not Sarah's and Hagar's. Abraham is the prototype of the man of faith whose surrender to divine will and godly hospitality entitles him to become the progenitor of a new nation chosen to serve the one God.

Sarah becomes the mother of the Israelites and Hagar the mother of the Ishmaelites. It is a tragedy that religion and ideology have transformed this story into a conflict of faiths and peoples. The ultimate irony is the consequent suffering of the hundreds of thousands of women and children who have died as a result of religious and national wars fought in the name of this text.

Let us give honor to the origins of our people by reframing the story. Let us stand together against the abuse of children and women in the name of religion. Women, let us extricate our peoples from the patriarchal borders that make it impossible to see one another as sisters sharing a common bond. We can no longer afford to place our children on the bloody altars of Abraham's faith or raise the knife above our children's heads. We must scream, cry, and protest holy wars and national struggles that do not grant basic recognition of the humanity of the other.

The prayer that follows is to be recited during Rosh HaShanah when we as a people try to come into harmony with all our relations and pray to renew our commitment to living with compassion. On Rosh HaShanah we also begin to prepare ourselves for Yom Kippur, which is a day dedicated to forgiving and seeking forgiveness. *Achti*, which means "my sister" in Arabic, is Sarah's formal apology to Hagar. However, apologies are meaningless if they are not followed by actions intended to repair the damage. I hope this prayer encourages Jews and Palestinians to acknowledge our common humanity and end the violence between our peoples. Women's voices must become the voice of the shofar blown at Rosh HaShanah. The voice of the shofar, some say, was the voice of Sarah calling out to Abraham: Do not harm the child in any way! The *tekiah* is a wake-up call, an alarm, a cry. Rather than side with the political and religious ideologies of our husbands, we must sound the alarm that emanates from our common motherhood: Do not harm our children in any way!

ꙮ *Achti*

Achti
I am pained I did not call you
By the name your mother gave you.
I cast you aside,
Cursed you with my barrenness and rage,
Called you stranger, ha-gar,
As if it were a sin to be from another place.
Achti
They used me to steal your womb,

Claim your child,
As if I owned your body and your labor.
I, whom they call See Far Woman,
Could not witness my own blindness.
But you, my sister,
You beheld angels,
Made miracles in the desert,
Received divine blessings from a god,
Who stopped talking to me.
Only at the end,
When I witnessed my young son screaming under his
*   father's knife,*
Only then
Did I realize our common suffering.
And I called out, Avraham, Avraham, hold back your
*   knife!*
My voice trumpeted into the silence
of my sin.
Forgive me, Achti
For the sin of neglect
For the sin of abuse
For the sin of arrogance
Forgive me, Achti,
For the sin of not knowing your name.

BUFFALO WOMAN RIVKEH

Rebecca, or Rivkeh, is a main character in the story of Jacob. She merits becoming the bride of Isaac by drawing water for a stranger and his camel. The stranger is Eliezer, servant of Abraham, who offers her marriage into his family. The choice of her as Isaac's bride rests on a trait that the Bible values most: hospitality to strangers.

As Rebecca heads toward a new household and a new land, the women of her household play the frame drum, dance, and sing to her, wishing her well. Her going forth is described in the same language as Abraham and Sarah's.

Rebecca marries Isaac and becomes pregnant. This time the struggle for inheritance rights is between, not two mothers and their sons, but twin brothers, who begin their struggle in her womb. Rebecca seeks divine guidance, presumably from a sacred site, where YHVH speaks to her directly and tells her what is to come.

She struggles to fulfill God's preference for her younger son. The elder twin, Esau, is red and hairy—a redneck?—and a hunter. The younger, Jacob, herds sheep and stays close to home. But Isaac prefers the hunter and makes ready to give him the blessing of land.

Rebecca, like coyote, the Native American trickster, deceives her husband by dressing her younger son in his brother's clothes and covering his hands and arms with goat hair. But was she really intending to deceive him? Knowing her husband, did she assume he would understand her cryptic message to bless this son instead? The story is unclear about this.

Esau is furious when he learns what his brother has done and threatens to kill him. Rebecca sends Jacob away, and his spiritual journey begins in earnest. We do not meet Rebecca again. Once she has fulfilled her role in the drama of Jacob, she is no longer necessary to the tale.

There are so many stories about sons. I asked myself, What if Rivkeh had given birth to twin daughters instead of sons? What if daughters, not sons, had furthered the plot of divine blessings on the people? I also wondered about the meaning of Rivkeh's name, since no explanation is given in the text. Perhaps understanding the meaning of her name would give me a direction for a story.

Rivkeh is derived from a word meaning "noose" or "lariat" used by herding peoples to control their animals. I began to think of Rivkeh as Buffalo Woman and to consider the spiritual dimensions of wild cattle in her society.

As is often the case with early Hebrew literature, the tales of women are better understood if we know their connection to ancient Goddess stories. The wild cow was a symbol of the Goddess in the ancient Near East. For many peoples, animals possess both an earthly and at the same time numinous quality. They reflect aspects of the sacred in physical form.

Rivkeh suddenly became *riv-kau, kau* being the Egyptian word for cow. Even though Rivkeh comes from Mesopotamia, the connection stimulated my midrashic mind. Wild cow's milk and milky way, horned crescent is the shape of the moon, her powerful bellow is the voice of the Creator.

Archaeological evidence also added a piece to Rivkeh's story. In the ruins of Kuntillet Ajrud, in the eastern Sinai, which date from the eighth century B.C.E., a drawing of YHVH as the bull god and Asherah as a cow goddess has been discovered. Asherah was the Canaanite Mother of the gods. Wasn't Rivkeh also grandmother of our people? The importance of the cow as a representation of the divine can be gauged from its association with idolatry. In the story of the golden calf, it is a cow that the Israelites choose to fashion to express their devotion to YHVH. The first letter of the Hebrew alphabet (א) is also an icon of a cow! The cow is walking westward, and our view is looking down at the top of the cow. The first letter of the alphabet from the perspective of Torat HaShekinah honors Rivkeh, whose fierce love can be compared to the wild cows.

I decided to write a story about Rivkeh as mother of twin daughters. Perhaps this story occurred when her sons went off and her husband died. I called her daughters Asherah and Anat. Asherah, a marine goddess, is the Mother of the gods and wife of El in the Ugaritic pantheon. She is symbolized by the tree of life in the form of a seven-branched menorah. The Israelites appropriated the seven-branched menorah as one of the four sacred objects placed in their temples. Anat is the Canaanite Goddess who is sister to Baal and a fierce and mighty warrior. In her own epic, Anat secures a permanent residence for her brother, Baal, by intimidating her father, El, who is head of the pantheon. Then she goes to battle in his behalf and defeats his foes. I have adopted these two names to indicate the strength and fearlessness of Rivkeh's two daughters. Here, then, is the tale.

These are the generations of Rivkeh, daughter of one whose name is not known, daughter of Milcah.

An old woman approached the well in the heat of the day, straining under her load. Many were drawing water there. Rivkeh, who is Buffalo Woman, raised her eyes and ran to greet the old one.

"Grandmother, drink from my pitcher and quench yourself." Rivkeh took the woman's burden and led her to the shade of a palm. Then she knelt down and gave the woman to drink.

"Grandmother, come with me and spend the night. Be my honored guest."

So the two of them set forth, and Rivkeh carried the old woman's burden. When they came to her tent, Rivkeh tended to the old woman. She washed her feet, gave her cool drink, prepared a meal of flat bread, goat cheese, olives, figs, honey cake, and date wine. All that she had she offered the old one.

It was the moon of the longest night.

The old one drew a pomegranate from her sack and opened it.

She gave Rebecca two seeds. "Eat this, my daughter, and it will be well with you."

Buffalo Woman ate. In the morning the old woman continued on her way.

It happened in the moon of the sap rising that Rivkeh ceased her flowing. She went to inquire of the elderly Devorah. Talking Bee Woman placed Rivkeh in the middle of the circle of stones, put her hands on Rivkeh's belly, and felt new life growing there.

"Two daughters will be born of your womb. They will walk in harmony, and the elder will save the younger."

Rivkeh stayed with Talking Bee and slept in the dream circle in the center of the stones.

And Rivkeh saw a white buffalo grazing by the bend in the river. Alongside the buffalo was a wild red mare and a raven black as night.

Rivkeh awoke. "Behold, I have seen a vision." She poured oil over the stones and pronounced a blessing for the gift of seeing given unto her.

And it came to pass in the moon of the almond blossoms that Rivkeh bore two daughters. One had long red hair like the mane of a wild mare. The other was slender and dark with fingers delicate as feathers.

They emerged from Rivkeh's womb hand in hand.

The red-haired sister she called Anat. The dark one she called Asherah, saying, "My heart overflows with joy because of the birth of my two daughters."

Anat grew to become a cunning hunter. Asherah herded goats and sheep. Yet they walked with one spirit and were seldom apart.

Rivkeh loved her daughters equally. They dwelled in one tent. But Rivkeh's heart was troubled because of Devorah's words "the elder will save the younger."

In the winter of their sixteenth year Anat set out to hunt venison. Asherah stayed by their tent and cooked lentils in a pot, for she knew her sister would be hungry upon her return.

Asherah heard the neigh of a stallion and looked up. Before her was a mighty warrior. He carried a sword of iron and rode an Egyptian horse. Asherah saw by his dress that he was a man who hired himself to kings and chieftains in exchange for the privilege of looting.

That day the man who was known as Tertzach came upon Asherah sitting by her tent and said, "I am nearly faint with hunger. Feed me lest I die."

She fed him, but he was not appeased. Tertzach seized Asherah and carried her off upon his horse.

Her cries brought Buffalo Woman running, but he was already beyond the flight of her arrow.

Rivkeh set out to find her daughter Anat. She tracked Anat to the hill country to the north.

"Your sister has been abducted!"

Together they set out. Buffalo Woman and her daughter followed the course of the wadi and Tertzach's tracks. Behold, they raised their eyes and saw a white buffalo grazing by the bend in the river.

When Rivkeh saw the wild cow nursing its calf, she lifted up her voice and cried. The cry brought Tertzach to a halt, and he rode to investigate. Rivkeh and Anat hid in the grass, for they heard bells tied to his steed, and Anat unleashed her arrow, which pierced Tertzach in the thigh and caused him to tumble from his horse, which fled.

When Tertzach beheld the three women standing by the banks of the river, he fell on his own sword rather than endure the shame of his limping defeat.

Then Rivkeh, Asherah, and Anat returned to their tent with Terzach's gold and booty, which they distributed among the people. Their deeds of courage became a song among the women at the well.

SOFT EYES WOMAN, LEAH

Leah is the eldest daughter of Rebecca's brother Lavan, who tricks Jacob into marrying his undesirable eldest daughter. Just as Rebecca disguised Jacob to deceive Isaac, so Lavan disguises Leah on her wedding day, and Jacob marries her thinking she is his beloved Rachel.

Leah's success at bearing Jacob sons does not win his love, although she is buried alongside him in the ancestral burial cave. The biblical text attempts to portray Leah's anguish over Jacob's indifference to her when it explains the names of her sons (e.g., Reuben and Levi, Genesis 29:32–34). Yet, once again, we are not given a full or complex picture of this foremother. The text doesn't bother to include Leah's reaction to the rape of her only daughter, Dinah.

My reflections on the story of Leah brought to mind women who are able to derive a sense of self-worth only from the approval they receive from men. Leah was cursed with ugliness in the story, and so she was not able to draw her husband to her. Many women are obsessed with their appearance, a fixation on the outer that comes from society's preference for attractive women. Endless dieting and anxiety about avoiding male displeasure are overarching themes in the lives of many women. The poem about Leah that follows speaks to the destructive effects of women's valuing ourselves by a standard that is not rooted in the beauty within.

Leah's Anguish

With years of child after child after child
Leah resembled a milk cow.

She lumbered heavily on swollen feet;
Skin hung from her body in folds;
Her eyes protruded from her flesh,
Pits of denied love.
He rarely came,
And when he did
It was over before it began.
He would not till her fields
Or plow her soil
Or plant honeysuckle kisses on her lips.
He merely groaned and fled,
Leaving her with endless tears of frustration.
To him, she was silage.
So she ate,
She ate her husband's food
Her children's food
Her father's food.
She picked at their fodder,
Lapped up honey from earthen jars.
She ate while preparing food,
Between meals, and when she cleaned up.
She sewed pockets on her clothing
So she could carry bread and fruit.
Pieces of dried meat stuck to her teeth,
Flies swarmed about her mouth.
She consumed endlessly so as not to feel the rising hunger
That gnawed at her body and laid waste her heart.
She gave birth to child after child
But none of them satisfied the devouring rage

That fed on her desperation.

So she grew big as a cow,

Lost in her own flesh

Until she died of consumption,

Never knowing

The rewards of being the fertile wife.

RACHEL

Rachel, daughter of Lavan and sister to Leah, is the beautiful younger daughter whom Jacob loves. She falls in love with Jacob, and Lavan promises to permit the marriage in exchange for seven years of Jacob's labor. On their wedding night, however, Jacob, who deceived his elder brother through disguise, is himself deceived through disguise and mistakenly marries Leah, the ugly elder sister.

The Bible does not tell us the details of this deception but cryptically remarks, "Behold, in the morning it was Leah." Because it speaks from Jacob's point of view, we, like him, are left in the dark with our imagination. Different ways of telling the untold story of the deception emerge in Talmudic and midrashic literature and continue to be told to this day.

Through a series of more deceptions Jacob acquires many possessions, including two wives, twelve children, and livestock. At this point Jacob notices that Lavan and his sons are unhappy about Jacob's success, and YHVH commands Jacob to return home. After consulting Rachel and Leah, Jacob flees without informing Lavan. But Lavan overtakes him and then permits him to leave with his daughters and acquired goods once Lavan realizes (by means of a dream) that God is on Jacob's side. Jacob is, after all, his sister's son. The wily Jacob once more slips through with his life and property intact. But not the women.

In the only instance of a unified voice between them, both Rachel and Leah accuse their father of stealing their inheritance. They therefore have no choice but to remain under the protective umbrella of Jacob, who shows signs of being able to deliver their children a landed inheritance. But Rachel steals *teraphim* (which I would translate as "those forbidden things"), which are apparently fertility figurines, since she is pregnant with her second son and elderly and seeks protection from a familiar source. The beloved Rachel, however, dies in childbirth in Bet Lechem, a cultic site I would translate as the "Shrine of the Bread." The teraphim do not save her, and her death in the story is a veiled punishment for reliance on foreign gods.

Jacob had taken an oath to his God YHVH, swearing fidelity and promising death to those in his family who relied on other gods. Rachel bears the burden of that oath, for in deceiving her father by sitting on the idols and pretending she could not rise up to greet her father because of her menses, she also deceives her husband, who had uttered the oath without knowing that his wife retained statues of the Goddess in the form of fertility figurines.

With her last breath she names her son Ben Oni, "Son Who Caused My Suffering." Jacob names the child BenYamim, "Son of My Later Years."

Rachel retained the voice of lamentation and protest as a principal characteristic of her ongoing midrashic persona. The site of Rachel's grave seems to have been known in Jeremiah's time, and it continues to be treated as a pilgrimage shrine to this day. The stories people tell about Rachel follow the same motif as stories told about the Virgin Mary. She is seen as the intercessor spirit, the suffering woman who is able to transform God's harsh decrees—based on strict interpretation of his law according to the principle of appropriate punishment for transgressions—to acts of compassion and forgiveness.

Over time a legend was told to explain how God allowed the return of the exiles after a relatively brief absence from the land, which was intertwined with a story explaining the way in which Jacob was deceived on his wedding night.

✑ *Rachel's Lament*

A voice was heard in Ramah
Lamentations and bitter weeping.

Rachel weeping for her children.
She refuses to be comforted because they are not.
Thus says YHVH
Refrain thy voice from weeping,
Thine eyes from tears,
For your work shall be rewarded
And your children shall come home again
From the land of the enemy.

When the Holy Temple was destroyed, the people of Israel were cast out of their homes, out of their tribal lands. The families who served the Temple, the families who served the king, the families of the tribes of Ephraim and Manasseh, Yehuda and Benyamin, and the remnant of the ten tribes exiled by the Assyrians—all our people from elder to infant were forced to walk from the holy land to the nation of Bavel. With their homes afire, their holy city in ruins, the people wept as they left their homes in chains.

They walked past the grave of our mother Rachel, mother to the tribes of Ephraim, Manasseh, and Benjamin. Her descendants cried out to her, and Rachel heard their prayers.

It is said among our people that the Holy One has two thrones in the heavenly chambers: One is the throne of divine love and compassion, the other is the throne of divine justice. In the last days of the Temple of God, a harsh decree had fallen upon the people because of the idolatry of that generation. All our holy ancestors gathered before God in the halls of heaven to protest. A great multitude of sages and holy prophets and kings, patriarchs and unborn souls amassed in front of the divine throne to plead for the people Israel. Each holy soul offered its own purest deed of love to awaken compassion in the divine heart, to no avail.

Then Rachel stepped forward and began to speak:

"I would like to remind you of the time I learned my sister was to be married to Jacob in my stead. Jacob and I devised signs by which we would know each other on our wedding night. If he did not consummate the marriage with my sister, then he would not be legally married. But at the last moment, I saw that my sister would be shamed, and I surrendered my jealousy for her sake. We got Jacob drunk, and I concealed myself under the marriage couch and spoke for my sister while her marriage was consummated, for otherwise no one would marry her. If I, who am dust and ashes, surrendered my jealousy and acted with compassion, cannot the Creator of the universe, the Compassionate One from whom we learn compassion, forgive your children and restore them to their home?"

Rachel took up her lament, and she wept for her children.

Then, before the eyes of all the hosts of heaven, Shekinah arose from the throne, gathered all the homeless ones under her wing, and carried them home.

In the story of Rachel, the images of exile, feminine presence, lamenting women, and the community of Israel merge. The beloved wife and mother convinces the Patriarch of Heaven to act as a loving father. She brings out the best in God.

Jacob wrestles his brother's guardian spirit and faces directly that which caused his original flight. His name change, to Israel, reflects his success. He has overcome his fear and embraced it in the light of truth. Rachel, by contrast, is killed by the very thing she yearned for her entire life: the birth of a child. Her guardian spirits do not save her; her spiritual possessions cause her death.

Jewish legend reimages Rachel, not as the mother who cursed her son with her last breath, but as a compassionate mother interceding on behalf of her children. She has learned compassion through the agency of her sister Leah, who is akin to the forgotten underworld princess Ereshkigal. Rachel, like Inanna, is revived to hero status by demonstrating her capacity for love under siege when she chooses her sister's welfare over her husband's. This act is the seed of her new identity. Unlike Jacob, Rachel never receives a new name for her heart transformation. Perhaps, like not a few Jewish women I have met in my travels, women can name our daughters Leah-Rachel and in so doing let one woman honor both names. Unlike their father, mother, and husband, we do not have to choose between them.

9

The Freedom Generation

THE TORAH TELLS the story of a people, Israel, who became slaves and were redeemed by the hand of God, who performed miracles in their behalf. It is the courage of midwives, however, that advances the plot. Their resistance allows the story to unfold. Six women are named as midwives in Jewish legends: Serach, Shifra, Puah, Yocheved, Miriam, and Elisheva. They are named because of their acknowledged contribution in the process of redemption.

Nonsexist Judaism must be committed to telling the fullest possible versions of the women's stories when we retell the exodus legends, since this event is our tale of origins. The people of Israel based the laws of their new society upon the foundation of this event: "We were slaves in the land of Egypt. Therefore, do not oppress a stranger, for you know the heart of a stranger, because we were slaves." I would like to weave together existing legends and flesh out the stories of Serach, Yocheved, and Miriam as principal characters in the story of our freedom.

SERACH

Nothing but Serach's name appears in the biblical exodus story, but many legends have accrued to her name. As a young girl, her skill at playing the lyre and composing songs leads her uncles (Joseph's brothers) to employ her services when they must reveal to Jacob that Joseph is still alive. She goes to her grandfather's tent and plays comforting music to relax his mind, and then, with her craft, she delivers the news. We find her again in her status as crone, living in Egypt, the last survivor of the family who had originally migrated there.

Serach knows the whereabouts of Joseph's bones. Pharaoh had thrown them into the River Nile to impede the exodus of the Israelites, but Serach raises them up in order that Joseph may be buried in his mother's land. When Moses returns from the wilderness proclaiming himself the spokesperson of God, it is Serach whom he must convince first to obtain the backing of the elders.

In the legends Serach, like Elijah, does not die. When the seas part for the Israelites, she ascends to heaven and lives on in the stories of Jews as the old one who comes to earth from time to time to see if we need extra help. And we always do!

Every Passover I invite Serach to the seder. We dress someone (usually me) in an old woman's mask. Serach enters grumbling. "Santa Claus gets to ride in a sleigh, and Elijah taxis through the universe on a flaming chariot, but *I* have to hobble around without vehicular transportation." Then she makes a crack about the lousy public transportation system in Albuquerque. The buses stop running after 8:00 P.M., and she has to hitch a ride to our Seder. She asks if anyone is willing to drive her home. Usually a few people volunteer. Then Serach settles down to tell a story on the theme of women who are brave in the face of danger.

> *I am the withered old scroll*
> *Whose flesh bears testimony to the years.*
> *I am a story crone, full of memories and details.*
> *I can look at you and see what you are rooted to.*

I know things.

I, Serach, am a grinder of corn.

In Egypt the young women of Israel would come to me, and I would teach them how to grind and bake the flour, mix the water, and bake the bread. I tell them, "This is how you survive: Remember the name your people have given you, remember the language you spoke as a child, and remember the time of the holy days of your people and you will endure."

When the sea parted, the people say I turned into an eagle and flew up to heaven to guide them across the sea toward the promised land. My wings were golden; some said I looked like the sun. I still fly about to talk to my children on this great day that recalls our birth as a people. I've come to tell you a story. Do you know about . . .

. . . and a story begins.

SHIFRA AND PUAH

Shifra and Puah are mentioned in Exodus chapter 1 as midwives who served the Israelites. Their part in the story of liberation is profound, because they were the first line of resistance to Pharaoh. Their commitment is to life, to children, to freedom. We are not clearly told if they are Israelites or Egyptians. Our spiritual and physical liberation was made possible by women who enabled other women to give birth by assisting them in their labor. Shifra and Puah are catalysts; they engender response; they defend the needs of laboring woman.

I perceive the passage in Exodus dealing with the midwives as a song:

⇌   *A Song for the Midwives*

V'yatev Elohim l'miyaldot

Va'yehrev ha-am v'ya'atzmu m'od

Vay-he ki yaru ha-m'yaldot et Elohim

Va-ya-as lahem batim batim.

Allspirits Elohim did well with the midwives.

The people multiplied and increased.

Because the midwives loved Elohim

They were granted ongoing generations.

YOCHEVED

Yocheved, the mother of Miriam, Aaron, and Moshe receives little attention in the Bible or in postbiblical legends other than the description of her as a midwife. I began to research her name, which intrigued me. *Yo-Cheved* means "YHVH's glory." Cheved is associated with the cloud of glory that was a sign of YHVH's presence. In mystical writings this cloud of glory became identified with the Shekinah. I decided to translate her name "Golden Cloud Woman" in honor of Shekinah's light in her name.

One of the folk motifs associated with the Shekinah is similar to the story of Cinderella. Shekinah, like Cinderella, is cast out of her royal home and must dwell among the ashes. Her kindness and suffering eventually lead to her restoration to the throne she rightly deserves to inherit. A beautiful but little-known part of the Cinderella story tells of her visiting the grave of her mother. She plants a tiny hazel sprig over the grave and cries over it every day. The tree miraculously grows and shades her. One day a bird comes to dwell in the tree and subsequently grants her secret wishes. One day she hugs the tree, and a light rises up from the roots and surrounds them both with its illumination. The bird begins singing and flies around the tree. Later in the story her fairy godmother appears to grant her wishes once again.

This portion of the Cinderella story somehow spoke to me as I reflected on Golden Cloud Woman. The following story of Yocheved blends the motifs in the exodus story with those suggested by the affinity between the Shekinah legend and the story of Cinderella. I created a genealogy that preserved separate identities for Shifra and Yocheved and made them mother and daughter.

A new pharaoh who did not know Yosef arose over Mitzryim. He said to his people, "Look, the Israelites are too numerous and too strong for us. We must deal cleverly with them now before their numbers increase even more and they join forces with our enemies and drive us from our own land."

So they appointed taskmasters over us to crush our spirits with hard labor. We were forced to build the storage sites of Pithom and Ramses as supply centers for Pharaoh.

But the more they oppressed us, the more we increased.

They came to dread us.

They forced us to do labor designed to break our bodies.

They made our lives miserable with harsh work involving mortar and brick as well as all kinds of toil in the field.

Pharaoh summoned the head midwives of the Evreem to his court. That is the name they called us, Evreem: vagabonds and wayfarers.

My mother was one of the midwives. The people called her Shifra: Horn of Freedom Woman. She turned each birth into a celebration. Somehow she collected wine and bread, shells and beads, goat hair blankets, and baskets woven from the tall grass by the river. We would gather and rejoice in the new child and renew our hope.

Pharaoh could not sleep. On the nights the Israelite women gave birth he dreamt of grasshoppers, swarming insects, and frogs crawling over his face and hands. While the women groaned with labor he screamed his midnight fears into the darkness of Mitzryim.

He summoned my mother, Shifra, saying, "When you deliver a Hebrew infant, if it is a boy, smash its head on the birth stone; if it is a girl, let it live."

My mother did not do as Pharaoh commanded.

One day they came for her and hanged her from a tree. I watched as they buried my mother's body, and I planted a cedar twig over her grave. Every day I would visit her and weep. Because I came so often and cried so much the twig quickly grew into a tree.

One day a white dove nested in the tree, and I took it as a sign. Soon the bird ate from my hand and cooed a welcome when I came.

One evening under a full moon sky I embraced the tree and felt the warmth of my mother's light rising, her spirit ascending, and the bird flew about us, cooing, and a voice spoke to me saying, "I am the Presence that sustained your mothers and fathers and promised them freedom. I am Shekinah, who will lead the people from darkness to light, from sorrow to joy, from slavery to redemption. From this time onward you shall be called

Golden Cloud Woman, for you have seen the light of Shekinah. Let My light become a sign of hope among the people."

My tears watered the tree once again, and I returned home.

From that time onward the people called me Yocheved for the golden cloud that surrounded me. It was a great sign of hope. The days of deliverance were at hand.

MIRIAM

Miriam means both "Mistress of the Sea" and "Bitter Waters Woman." I have translated her name "Parting Seas Woman" to indicate the event for which she is best known, that is, leading the women in a victory dance after Israel's miraculous salvation. The double meaning of her name represents the double-edged experience of the Jewish people, our bitterness and our joy. Bitterness arises from the memories of our suffering. Joy is a spiritual quality we have cultivated, which can transform bitterness into endurance, creativity, and love.

Miriam's story is sparsely told. Her nurturing role as sister is stressed over her creative role as seer and prophet. The fact that she is called the sister of Aaron and not the sister of Moshe suggests an independent tradition for Miriam. Miriam and Aaron were possibly cultic figures in their own right representing different traditions of priestly and oracular clan centers whose stories were blended with the folk hero tales of Moshe to create an integrated tale about leaving Egypt. Numbers 12 especially reflects the Bible's prejudice against Miriam's claim to speak in the name of YHVH. For her assertion that God also speaks to her, Miriam is given a case of leprosy. Her challenge to Moshe's exclusive right to relate the word of YHVH to the people brings about her demise.

I wanted to recover Miriam's voice as wise elder, so I sat down to my typewriter in my tiny Sixty-fourth Street apartment in New York City while the lions in the zoo roared one morning. I wrote a story about

Miriam's response to the denial of her power of vision. By noon I was
covered with a red rash, like Miriam the leper! The next month I told the
Rosh Hodesh group in Philadelphia, with whom I celebrated, about my
rash and sang them the songs I wrote for Miriam. I am one of those
American Jewish women who was never given a Yiddish or a Hebrew
name. The women of Rosh Hodesh felt that my experience with the
story of Miriam, my gifts as a storyteller, and my life as a woman rabbi
were a sign that I should take on the name Miriam. They created a little
ceremony and officially bestowed it on me. I have kept that name to this
day and cherish the circle of women who filled the void created by my
family, who ceased to pass on the naming traditions to their daughters.

These are the songs and stories I have written about Parting Seas
Woman, Miriam.

Song to Miriam

Miriam drew her brother out of the river.
Miriam sang open the waters of the sea.
Miriam saw God as a midwife woman.
Miriam brought the desert her well of waters.

Once we were nothing,
dust in Pharaoh's eye,
Until she came
Like the raging sea
And washed our wounds.
In the healing waters of her courage
We found our tongues
Singing in our mouths.
When the midwives chanted
Over Golden Cloud's womb
On the day she sought the birth oracle

They foresaw her coming. They sang:
She will come like a midwife woman
With her curing herbs
Healing our troubles away.
She will come like a pride of lions
Fierce in the hunt
Holding her enemies at bay.
She will come like Buffalo Woman
Snorting back the waters,
Leading the herd through the pass.
She will come like a high-flying eagle
Soaring to the promised land,
Where she can rest at last.

Miriam's Prayer for Her Mother

Her voice wet and open
crying like a jackal in the night,
a storm raging inside her
the rage of Yehoyah
She sees the tear-stained women
hiding themselves in the fields,
squatting over stones,
stifling their birth cry,
The blood between their legs rising to Yehoyah's nostrils.
Miriam lifts her voice
And prays with her mother:
"No more dead children.
This boy shall live!"

Miriam's Teachings

My kin,
we build pyramids for hollow men,
our sides ache,
we destroy our bodies from work,
wreak havoc upon our souls.
Do the gods of our oppressors heal our children
or comfort our grief?
We serve Mitzryim with our lives,
carve their idols out of carob wood,
fashion ornaments of turquoise for their rich
and clear their way up the river to the tombs.
They cover the path with the bodies of our children;
they rule over us,
embitter our lives.
Awake, awake,
Yehoyah's children!
Declare a day of feasting.
Yehoyah calls us
To serve Her in the wilderness.
Yehoyah summons us
to freedom.
Set a table for the needy.
Offer our miserable bread to the homeless.
She will bear us on eagle wings
to a place where freedom
swells up like a mighty river,
where joy rises like a swiftly flowing stream.
Brothers and sisters, the day of freedom is upon us.

Song at the Sea

Sing to Yehoyah, whose glory thunders.
All the mighty warriors drown in the sea
Which gave us birth.

Miriam's Well

The storytellers say
Women from thirteen tribes would gather at Miriam's well
and call to the waters:
Rise up, well waters, rise,
and the waters would rise and overflow.
The women would visit each other in boats
traveling on Miriam's waters.
The storytellers say
Miriam's well could cure the sick and heal
  the brokenhearted
if they drank before three stars emerged as Shabbat ended.
The storytellers say
Miriam's well provided water for the people
during their long sojourn in the wilderness.
When Miriam died,
she bequeathed her power to find water
to the women who sang with her at the sea.

River Song

I'm standing at the edge of a great river
Flowing to the mouth of God.
Carrying me singing to the river,
She is in my song.

THE NEED FOR NEW STORIES

We need to tell the story of all the women again. We need to become storytellers, able to spin compelling yarns, to replace the countless cartoons and commercials with legends connected to the themes embedded in the old tales: the courage to face our fears, the choosing of good over evil, the need for hospitality, the wisdom of elders as a source of knowledge, the knowledge that allows us to overcome our suffering, heal our wounds, and create a life of joy.

Part Three

↩ CEREMONY

DISCOVERING THE ROOTS OF
JEWISH WOMEN'S CEREMONY

Judaism is a tradition rooted in ceremony, but Jewish women have been silent partners in conducting and interpreting holy days. There are so many tales of exclusion.

I was in Amsterdam attending a Yiddish theater festival. The first Saturday morning, my new friend Hankus Netzky and I decided to scout out the city's Jewish section. We wove through narrow streets lined with canals and four-hundred-year-old buildings. Finally we came upon the magnificent Portuguese synagogue compound and entered its hidden courtyard. We were guided to a tiny chapel by two young Israeli security guards. Hankus stayed downstairs with the men while I mounted the narrow steps to the women's section.

I peered at the scene below. Men, old and young, were singing, praying, and schmoozing. The leader of the prayers was a young red-headed fellow sporting a formidable black top-hat in the fashion of Portuguese Jews. With busy familiarity, he davened his way to the completion of the morning service. Beside me in the small women's section sat a young woman about the same age as the leader of prayer, gazing shyly through the wooden lattice at her male relatives below. Later she served us cake. To her belonged the task of cooking and serving food, bearing sons, and sitting quietly above, away from the Torah, her head covered with a wig. To the young man belonged the honors of Bar Mitzvah, leadership of prayers, a public voice in communal affairs, and a top hat. When Hankus informed one of the younger men who chatted with us that I was a rabbi, our guide leaned over and whispered, "Better not tell any-body here!" Although I try not to feel too much resentment in these sit-uations, I wonder how different it would be for this congregation if the young girl next to me were downstairs leading the prayers and the boy served cake. How would she think of herself then?

Ceremony is very important in Jewish tradition. Through the perfor-mance of ceremony we honor and observe the natural rhythms of our lives, such as birth, marriage, and death; we recall formative moments in our history and carry forward the values and ideals associated with those events; and we create bonds of community and culture, because our ceremonies regularly bring us together through the years.

While I was learning about women's exclusion from public ceremony in Orthodox circles, I began to uncover a rich history of Jewish ceremo-nial life practiced by women separately from the men. I first began to understand the scope of women's practices when I lived in Israel in the early 1970s. There I learned that Jewish women from Sephardic, Euro-pean, North African, and Middle Eastern communities possess a rich heritage of song, dance, storytelling, proverbs, and life cycle rituals.

For a brief period in 1970 I resided at a moshav on the Lebanese bor-der called Dovav. The residents of Dovav were Persian and Moroccan Jews. One evening I went with some of the Moroccan women to an en-gagement party. The food was delicious and the conversation animated, although I didn't understand much since they spoke in Arabic. When the bride-to-be entered the room, all the women threw candy at her and began emitting a piercing sound made from the throat. I was stunned. Their ululating was literally a far cry from the constrained melodies of the Reform choir I grew up with. That incident occurred before my introduction to feminism, and I had no knowledge of the long history of the women's ceremonial practices, to which ululating belongs. But the sound stayed with me.

After my formal initiation into feminism at the first Jewish Feminist Conference, I began to write stories for a theater company I created in 1975 called Bat Kol. We received our first opportunity to perform when my friend Rabbi Mel Gottlieb, an Orthodox Jew, told me that Rabbi Joseph Solevechik, a renowned Orthodox teacher, had canceled an engagement to speak before the M.I.T. Hillel, and Mel had no program to replace him. I told him my theater company (which had barely rehearsed) could be ready to perform in two weeks, and we would volunteer to take Rabbi Solevechik's place. Mel gave us the opportunity to perform Jewish feminist theater at M.I.T., and in two weeks Bat Kol presented five theater pieces: Sarah, Lilith, Deborah, the Apocalypse of Hannah, and the Secret Jew, a story about a conversa woman in Spain. At that performance I met my teacher Everett Gendler and his wife, Mary, who deeply influenced my relationship to Judaism. I will speak of them later. We were also reviewed by *Hadassah* magazine and on that basis were invited to perform in seven other places that year, including a retreat sponsored by the Jewish Feminist Organization.

Soon after our appearance at M.I.T., Elaine Shapiro and Eleanor Schick, the other members of Bat Kol, and I carpooled to upstate New York, braving icy roads and freezing weather. At that retreat I was introduced to Jewish women's ceremony by an Orthodox woman named Arlene Agus. After our performance Arlene lit candles floating in a clear glass bowl buoyed by a thin layer of oil and told us about an ancient and continuous woman's ceremony called Rosh Hodesh. I wondered at discovering yet another piece of women's culture in Judaism that had been shielded from my eyes. Growing up as a Reform Jew permitted me the opportunity to participate as an equal member of the Jewish prayer community, read from the Torah, and even compose liturgy. But I was not educated in women's practices, other than cooking holy day meals. Just as Judith Plaskow opened up the pathway to feminist storytelling, Arlene Agus opened the door to my study of women's ceremony in Judaism.

As my appetite for learning about women in Jewish culture grew, I sought out the company of other women scholars, researchers, artists, and storytellers and so came to know Penina Adelman. A folklorist, storyteller, and author of a book entitled *Riding the Nightmare*, Penina was attending a Rosh Hodesh group in Philadelphia. She convinced me to accompany her on the train and spend Rosh Hodesh Tevet with the group.

What a night! The New York Scholars in Religion did a lot of talking but no ceremony. The women who came to celebrate this recently re-consecrated time were in a mystical mood, ready to explore uncharted methods of expression. After lighting candles to a meditation written by Penina, we stood in two lines and birthed each other down a canal of women's hands, gently stroking one another's faces and humming as we crawled through. Our faces were washed at the end to mark our transition. Afterward we rose and danced in a circle chanting the letters Y-H-V-H.

Next we sat in a circle, and Penina passed around thirteen cards she had made out of colored construction paper. Each card represented a feminine mythic persona. Each woman chose the one that spoke to her and shared something about the image. Sheila Wienberg's card was Lilith. She held up the card and said that she would rather express her feelings through movement, and she suddenly began a birth dance on the floor. I shed the last remnant of my shyness about women's bodies in motion and began to sway and sing with Sheila, as did other women. My childhood training in creative dramatics prepared me to go with most any improvisation, and that night the ability to improvise in theater was expanded to ceremony. Women stayed late into the night. The excite-ment was palpable. By 2:00 A.M. four of us were sitting around the kitchen table, drinking herb tea and eating bowls of steamy oatmeal and orange slices while we chatted about our first sexual encounters, Jewish feminism, and the Shekinah. One of us wanted to know our astrological signs. Andy, Suri, Penina, and I each represented one of the four elements: earth, air, fire, and water. We laughed about it and took it as a good omen about the wholeness of spirit that dwelled in our hearts that night. Shekinah's Presence emerged through our creation of ceremony and awoke our forgotten knowledge.

RESTORING WOMEN TO CEREMONY

Part 3 is meant to help women make ritual, restore forgotten knowledge, and through this knowledge to feel whole.

The ceremonies that I will share with you in this book are dedicated to restoring women's ritual to normative status in synagogue and home life, and to the reinstatement of women as leaders of ritual. I have chosen to focus on a few representational ceremonies to help us reconstruct our ritual and ceremonial lives. Rituals orchestrate transitions in personal life. During such in-between periods, rituals help give order to our emotional responses, which might otherwise be experienced as chaotic. In this way rituals allow us to be creative and give design and beauty to our becoming.

Rituals can be ordered according to four basic stages:

1. What you are leaving behind.

2. What you take with you from the past.

3. What vision you hold of the new life you are about to enter.

4. Blessings offered by friends and community in honor of the initiate.

Ritual acts are symbolic enactments of feelings associated with each phase of transition. Leaving behind, for instance, can be represented by tearing up, burning, giving away, burying, or removing. Taking something with you can be expressed by adornment, bringing objects into a circle, tying knots. Future visions can be attended by oaths, vows, anointing with oil, or the taking of a new name. Blessings offered can take the form of words, gift giving, telling stories, and offering food to the person who is the focus of the ritual.

The first ritual is called the Mishkan ceremony. I composed it as a healing ritual for women based on the four directions of the wilderness tent called the Mishkan, which was the tribal shrine of the Israelites during their wilderness period.

The Mishkan ceremony is followed by a chapter devoted to women's four-thousand-year association with the consecration of the new moon. In recent times the celebration of Rosh Hodesh has served as a time and place for women to explore their spirituality, history, and identity as Jewish women. In the past twenty years hundreds of groups have sprung up throughout the United States, Europe, and Israel as Jewish women recover a holy day that had been in decline. This section provides a brief guide to the creation of twelve Rosh Hodesh ceremonies, one for each new moon in the lunar year.

I would also like to share ceremonies for Bat Mitzvah. I believe that the initiation of young girls into womanhood is essential for the preparation of the new Jewish woman who is confident about her place as a creative partner in her culture.

Many of the new rituals for Jewish women deal with birth. Yet I have found little material that helps women cope with the daily challenges of mothering. I have included a mother's daily prayer to help women renew themselves for the task of raising their children.

Finally I offer two ceremonies for women growing older so that their wisdom and life achievements can be publicly honored.

10
The Mishkan Ceremony

CURRENTLY MOST JEWISH practice is conducted by one person leading a congregation, which is seated and reading from a book. There are other possibilities.

When I was eight months' pregnant, I wanted to take my unborn son, Nataniel, to the corn dances at Cochiti Indian Pueblo. I drove with my friends Pat Jojola and Loren Kahn to visit friends of Pat's. We were served a huge meal of chili stew, Jello, potato salad, special Indian breads, and coffee, and we conversed with men who had served as forest rangers in the 1950s in New Mexico. Then we went out to watch the dance.

Our eyes scanned the perimeters of the village square for an unoccupied piece of ground. We found a spot and settled on the hard baked earth. I lost myself in the expanse of the gaudy turquoise skies, brown earth, and warm sun. The distant sound of drums beat against the air like birds in flight. Singers pounded wooden drum sticks against taut hides. Rows of dancers shaking rattles, bells, and shells slowly filled the square. Their reverence for the earth and the Creator touched my unborn child as a dance had once touched me. According to my mother and father, I was conceived after prayers for rain during their visit with my Uncle Dick, who lived in San Juan village in New Mexico. A picture of my mother washing her chestnut hair in a bowl outside my uncle's adobe house hangs near my desk as evidence of the tale.

As I sat on the ground at Cochiti and felt the rhythmic power of the dance in my body, I gave thanks for the endurance of Indian peoples upon the earth. Their ceremony continues to be a blessing for all who are privileged to participate. From the Indian communities of New Mexico, from the Pueblo peoples, the Hopi, Apache, and Navajo, I have learned new respect for ceremonies that honor the earth. They have taught me that ceremony that does not affirm our rootedness in the body of the earth cannot heal the wounds of our spirit or restore us fully to our human task in the world, which is to love life.

Native North and South American peoples have illuminated more earth-oriented religious practices in my own tradition. Our religion grew from a society of farmers and herders who viewed ethical behavior as the catalyst for the Creator's blessing of a fertile earth. Early Israelites also constructed shrines and lodges for the gods and goddesses who personified the forces of the natural and human world. Women as well as men conducted ceremony in those shrines. One such testimony to this is the answer of the women the prophet Jeremiah accused of bringing on the destruction of the first Temple in Jerusalem because of their religious practices. The women replied: "Since we left off burning incense to the queen of heaven and pouring out drink offerings to her, we lack all things and have been consumed by the sword and by famine. When we burned incense to the queen of heaven, poured out drink offerings and baked cakes to worship her with, did we do all this without our menfolk?" (Jeremiah 44:18).

From this we learn that women conducted ceremony for themselves and their husbands in local shrines throughout the land of Israel. The shrine, known as the Mishkan, that became the mythic prototype for the Temple in Jerusalem, was modeled on shrines once so accessible to women.

A BRIEF HISTORY OF THE MISHKAN

"Build me a Mishkan so I can abide with you." The Mishkan was a portable shrine that the Israelites transported from place to place during their journey in the wilderness. The building and dedication of the Mishkan take up four Torah portions, which are quite detailed and lengthy. The Mishkan housed ritual objects sacred to the people: the incense altar, a seven-branched menorah, the stone tablets of the covenant, the ark and cherubim, the table of twelve breads, the bowl of manna, and Aaron's staff. The tribes camped around the Mishkan, three tribes on each side radiating outward from the shrine like the rays of the sun. YHVH's presence would appear to the people as a golden cloud or a pillar of fire over the Mishkan. The description in the Bible reminded me of the sign of the Zia tribe of New Mexico, which is a sun with four rays emanating from four sides, representing the four directions.

The biblical descriptions of the Mishkan can be compared with excavated shrines from the period of the Judges and the early monarchy, after the people settled in the land, after 1200 B.C.E. These shrines were extremely small. People left animal, vegetable, and votive offerings to placate and honor the gods in hopes of receiving forgiveness or bounteous reward.

Shrines of the ancient Near East were sites honoring the goddesses as well as the gods. Women led ceremonies and transmitted the divine word. Biblical women such as Devorah (whose name is a title meaning "Oracle"), Miriam, and the wise woman of Avel most likely were heads of specific shrines. Shrines of the Goddess may have been viewed as the body of the Goddess herself, with the entrance representing her vagina, and the holy of holies, her womb. Another term for these shrines was *Beit*, meaning "Shrine of," followed by the name of the particular goddess or god, as in Beit El and Beit Anat. *Beit* belongs to the root for "house" and "wife" or "daughter." Shrines were originally modeled on women's homes. The shrine allowed women to invest with sacred meaning everyday activities such as lighting fire, baking bread, and washing as well as significant life passages such as birth and death.

As Shekinah evolved to a feminine divine presence in the imagination of the people, the Mishkan and then the Temple in Jerusalem also became Her home. In the legends, when the Temple was destroyed, the presence of Shekinah Herself became the protecting shelter of the Jewish people. The marriage huppah (canopy), the sukkah (fall harvest booth), and the tallit (prayer shawl) became, like the Mishkan, sanctuaries for the Shekinah. The root *Sh-K-n* refers to a nomadic sense of dwelling—the dwelling moves with the wanderer. The Shekinah wanders with the people. She provided them with sanctuary even during times of homelessness.

In the kabbala the mystic becomes the Mishkan of Shekinah. He prepares himself with prayer to become a vessel for Her to dwell within. The Mishkan ceremony I have created helps women also to become a Mishkan for the Shekinah.

Many Jews seeking new avenues of Jewish spirituality turn to the study of the kabbala. New Age Jewish teachers, who are often Orthodox men, teach "kabbalistic practices" supposedly based on authentic sources. As I previously discussed, I find the active male, receptive female notion of divine union on which this material rests an inhibiting proposition, especially given the victim status of the Shekinah as a ravaged woman unable to save herself. Moreover, the kabbala is based on medieval and Neoplatonic ideas of a ten-dimensional cosmos divided between the spiritual and material worlds, men and women, and true believers and heretics. Medieval teachers of kabbala fostered a trend away from the midrashic imagination of the classical period toward a very intellectualized system of divine life. And with a few brave exceptions, women were excluded from participating in kabbalistic circles of learning.

By turning to the Mishkan as a paradigm of healing for women, I am able to recover women's voices, which are still evident in the texts and archaeology of the early periods, and can reflect upon them as a source of inspiration for contemporary women. The Mishkan ceremony can be a source of kabbala for women by directing them to work toward a wholeness of spirit based on the receptive and active principles of feminine spirituality, which is lacking in traditional kabbala.

THE CEREMONY

The Mishkan ceremony is a ritual based on the four-directional nature of the Lodge. The Lodge is a term borrowed from Native American spirituality, which is based on the four directions. Each direction—east, south, west, and north—indicates a stage of passage toward wholeness of spirit. The east, represented by the incense altar, is the place we begin to purify ourselves for the ritual. The south, represented by the seven-branched menorah, deepens this process by focusing on the body's dance of energy. The west, represented by the stone tablets—both broken and whole—is a vision quest; and the north, represented by the twelve loaves of bread, is the place we share our vision in community. The Mishkan ceremony is a spiritual symphony composed of chanting, breath work, guided meditation, dancing, drumming, and storytelling. All these elements weave together a ceremony dedicated to reconsecrating our vision and to healing our wounded spirit. Before I give specific directions for creating a Mishkan ceremony, I would like to describe the context in which the ceremony was used.

A woman in her thirties came to me barely able to complete a sentence, backtracking over words, stuttering, endlessly repeating, "Sí, no, I don't know!" when trying to formulate an idea of what she meant to say. She was desperately searching for a resting place within herself from which she could learn to trust her voice. Her family, survivors of the European destruction of the Jews now residing in Buenos Aires, had invented a strategy to cope with the calamity wherein each adult member of the family would recount over and over again the stories of how they saved one another's lives. They would speak about nothing but their loyalty in the troubled times of the war. Meanwhile her mother's brother had been molesting her frequently, and she couldn't tell anyone. While everyone insisted on saying only good things about the family, her rage turned into madness, grief, and despair, and no one seemed to be able to see her suffering. She had fled her home and finally settled in Denver but was about to return to visit her mother, who had become quite ill. Fear overwhelmed her, shattering her confidence in her hard-won insights and her islands of inner strength. She arrived at my doorstep for a ceremony to give her strength to make the return.

We went to the Jemez Mountains, where the earth is iron red, where cottonwood, pine, and sage grow abundantly and natural hot springs gurgle alongside the river that flows there. Although it was winter, the mountains were warm. We hiked in toward the springs and found a secluded place under a canopy of ponderosa pines. We set up a little altar of objects she had brought along. She called her ceremony "She speaks what she sees." We faced the east, lit sagebrush, and prayed opening prayers that were composed spontaneously from the feelings in our hearts at that moment. She stated her intentions to be loyal to her own truth and to communicate that to her uncle. She was wary of confronting her mother with the reality of her childhood because of her mother's illness. She wanted to find the compassion to forgive her mother before she died. We turned to the south. She began to wail her grief, sweeping her hands back and forth through the pine needles, pushing them away to reveal the soft red earth underneath. We composed a chant as I shook a gourd rattle to name all the parts of herself that she loved. She finished each phrase saying, "I am eshet kallah, woman whole unto herself." As we faced west, I told her the story of the descent of Inanna into the underworld reframed as the descent of Eve to encounter Lilith, who represented Eve's totally free nature, her unafraid self, her lion woman. She helped tell the story, filling in moments of the story with great detail, especially the moment of Eve's rebirth! She was reborn with the spirit of Lilith in her heart. Lilith, the freedom of the night wind, scooped up Eve in her wings and, soaring to the heavens, taught her how to ride the currents that were like the wind inside her.

Then I played the dumbek to the Middle Eastern rhythm called *beladi,* a four-four rhythm to which women throughout the Middle East have danced the belly dance. She danced until she felt her energy strongly rooted in the earth; she stomped away her sadness and allowed her body to generate an erotic and revitalized energy flow until she began to ululate and twirl.

We lit sage once again and prepared ourselves for a mikveh, a ritual bath that purifies us for holy occasions. She wanted to purify herself for the journey. Jews have a tradition of making prayer before setting out on a journey, but mikveh is not usually associated with that practice. Here it seemed fitting. We entered the hot springs, and she performed the ritual of mikveh. She curled up in a fetal position under the water and allowed the water to touch her everywhere. She came up for air and went under again and then said the blessing, which she translated into a personal prayer for renewal. Then we relaxed in the water until twilight, when we headed back to the car and dinner.

The Mishkan ceremony allowed this woman to return home feeling stronger inside. She reported that her ritual helped her feel sane during her month-long stay. She returned ready to take up her life with renewed energy.

GUIDELINES FOR CREATING A MISHKAN CEREMONY

The goals of the ceremony are to develop inner strength, to heal our wounds, and to restore our knowledge of women's practices. The first step is giving ourselves permission to lead a ceremony that we ourselves compose. Creating ceremony allows us to experience ourselves in the role of wise woman healer, who is known by the Hebrew title *Hachama*. Learning how to conduct ritual can be compared with learning a craft or navigating life: It is a combination of inspiration and skill with details.

Mishkan is a portable shrine. As part of the ceremony we create a little shrine to Shekinah. A woman's Mishkan is a place she gathers all kinds of objects representing elements that are part of the sacred context of her life; she combines them into an artistic whole. The biblical Mishkan contained icons sacred to the people of Israel. Bring together items from your life and from the natural world that are sacred to you. Designate an area for the construction of the shrine. It can literally be a tent, the ground under a canopy of trees, a room in your house, the mikveh, or any other special place. Within that space create an altar for your special items. Use beautiful cloth, flowers, stones, family pictures, breads and fruits, incense, Grandma's jewelry—make it a place of beauty. The practice of using beautiful objects in the performance of ritual is called *hidur mitzvah.*

Choose a place that is secluded from the noise and bustle of the everyday world. Sacred space is accompanied by sacred time. Sacred time is that period set aside for the purpose of performing the ritual. In the space and place of the ceremony we are able to give ourselves over to the sacred task of healing and renewal.

Words, Actions, and Music

This particular ceremony is meant as a guide to help you create your own, which you should tailor to your needs. I have numbered the order of the service to help you follow the recipe.

1. *The ceremony begins with an invocation. A woman prays in song or speech:*

✦   *Invocation*

> *Shekinah, accept the ceremony of your people.*
> *Bless this Mishkan with your Presence.*
> *Receive our prayers and embrace them.*
> *Fill our hearts with compassion, understanding,*
>   *and peace.*

2. *An opening song is offered from Jewish women's folk music.* I would like to offer this song, which was influenced by Native American vocal styles I hear in the Southwest. The word I use for God in this song is *Yehoyah.* Yehoyah is the Shekinah in her aspect as midwife woman. She brings tenderness and love to creation. Her name is composed of the

Hebrew letters *yud, hay, vov, yud, hay,* which are the letters of YHVH. Yehoyah equals the numerical value of thirty-six, which is double *chai,* or "life." Yehoyah's double chai energy incorporates all polarities into an integrated whole. Her twin nature mirrors the helix that spirals forth new life. We place our prayers on the wings of Shekinah and have faith they will arrive at the right destination.

✧ *A Prayer to Yehoyah*

Yehoyah Spirit I seek your vision
Yehoyah Spirit I seek your grace
Yehoyah Spirit I seek your wisdom
Yehoyah Spirit I seek your peace
Fill me with your vision
Fill me with your grace
Fill me with your wisdom
Fill me with your peace.

3. *We turn toward the east, light incense, and meditate on the task of the day.* One woman leads a guided meditation for the east, which acts as an intention, or *kavanah,* for this direction. In Hebrew tradition the golden incense altar stood at the eastern entrance of the Mishkan. The east signifies the place of the rising sun, the dawn of new vision. We light incense on the altar to help us purify ourselves as we commence our prayers. Inhaling the aroma of the incense lets us establish ourselves in our sacred intention, bring ourselves to the present moment, and invoke our desire.

The woman who has called the ritual says: "Shekinah, I offer you a prayer of the heart and express my hope that you will guide me on my way. I [give your Jewish name], daughter of [give your genealogy, as many generations back in time you can go], stand ready to [name the sacred intention of the day and what you hope for]." She ends the prayer with "So may it be."

4. *We turn to the south and light a fire in an oil lamp* or put sand in a bowl and fill it with candles or build a small fire. Someone can read the following passage as an introduction for the south.

We turn to the south and remember the tree of life, symbolized by the seven-branched menorah. The menorah was originally the totem of the Goddess Asherah, Mother of gods, Lady of the Dancing Waves, Woman of the Rolling Hills. As we light the fires of this lamp we affirm our bodies as a reflection of her energy. We pick up the drum and the rattle, the bell and flute and begin to play the ancient melodies that fired women's spirits and caused them to find her presence in their own bodies through the dance. Let the dance open us to the powers of birth and death, our own powers of creation. As we move our hips and arms, as we breathe into our bellies, as we shake our bodies and stamp our feet, we dance with the earth and the wind and call upon our creative fires to heal our wounds and make us whole.

Women begin to play music and dance. I suggest that you use a simple rhythm played on percussion instruments to accompany the dance. You can use a mode called *Ahavah Raba,* or *hijaz,* both of which are Middle Eastern scales. Those who are interested in finding out more about Jewish women's music should find a teacher of dumbek and learn how to play the rhythm known as *beladi,* for this is the traditional rhythm of belly dancing. Belly dancing has survived thousands of years as a remnant of women's religion. There are over fourteen words for *dance* in the Bible, including dances that were associated only with women. The word *maholot,* for instance, meaning "round dance," appears only as a women's dance, as in "Miriam took the drum in her hand and all the women went out after her with frame drums and round dances" (Exodus 15:20). Jewish women from Middle Eastern cultures have kept the practice of belly dancing alive to this day. I have witnessed it in ceremonial contexts time and time again.

5. When the dancing has run its course, *we turn to the west and wash our hands in a ritual bowl of water.* A woman can read this passage, while shaking a rattle, as a guided meditation for the west:

Stones engraved with words spoken by the Creator were placed in a special wooden cabinet called the *aron*. Throughout the Near East the people drew pictures and wrote stories and laws on clay and stone, including stories of the goddesses. These special stones were stored in the holy of holies, and only the elder of the people could enter and make ceremony in the presence of those stones. The stones represent the wisdom of the people and so must be guarded by the most holy among them.

Today we don the mantle of the elder and enter the holy of holies that dwells within us. For we are like the Mishkan—Shekinah abides within us. Now we enter the holy of holies to seek out wisdom and bring it to light.

The sacred stones in the Mishkan are surrounded by objects that symbolize the elements of the life journey. To the right of the stones you will find the bowl of manna, which represents the eternal source of nourishment available to each human being. It contains the nourishment you have received in your life that sustains you in your journey. Look into the bowl. What nourishment is contained within? To the left of the stones stands the stick totem of Asherah, which is able to blossom and represents our ability to grow, bloom, and resurrect dead parts of ourselves. Imagine yourself holding the staff of life. It is a branch from Shekinah's tree. She gives it to you. You smell its sweet fragrance and touch places on your body that you wish to heal. Touch scenes in your life that you wish to heal.

The outer curtain of the ark is a tapestry of the night sky. We have to pass through the curtain of the night to receive the blessing hidden in the dawn. Imagine the face of the night through which you must pass to heal yourself. As you stand there facing the night, two fearsome lionesses emerge from the curtain to stand guard over the stones. These were originally the lions of Asherah, who rode them standing on their backs. They symbolize fierceness and courage in the face of death. Like the Goddess, you can stand upon the lions because you are unafraid. They are your allies in the search for deep wisdom.

Imagine yourself now entering the holy of holies. The lionesses curl up in the corner like house cats. Suddenly you are aware of the stones. They appear to be illuminated with a picture or a hieroglyph. You stare into a stone, which shines like a precious gem. It reveals to you the face of Shekinah. (At this point the rattle speeds up in rhythm.) As you gaze *panim el panim,* face-to-face, Shekinah speaks to you and gives you a gesture, a word, or a totem sign of the wisdom you need to carry back into the world. Breathe this wisdom into your being. And when you are ready, come stand before the entrance of the holy of holies and face north.

6. *Now an opportunity is provided for each woman to tell the others what she has learned from the ceremony.* One woman says: "In the north stood a table with twelve hallot, twelve round cakes offered by the twelve tribes. These loaves represent the spiritual nourishment of our collective

energies. Let us share the insights we gained from our meditations in the Mishkan as a way of increasing our blessings and wisdom."

Then an object that has been designated as the "talking stick" is passed from woman to woman, beginning with the woman who has called the ceremony, and each person shares part of her insight, until you have gone once around the circle. Each person speaks without being interrupted until everyone who so desires has a turn.

7. *The ceremony is concluded with a song.* One woman says, "In the north we shared those parts of the meditation that increased our understanding. Our insights are medicine to our spirits. Today we become healers. We use our wisdom to renew and strengthen us so we can walk in harmony upon the earth. We sing this song as a thanksgiving for the wisdom we have gained today."

Closing Song

I am a medicine woman,
A healer of souls.
I die and am reborn again
Six hundred thousand fold.

Heal me, open me,
Release my true heart song;
Lead me on the beauty way
My whole life long.

I am a medicine woman,
A healer of souls.
I walk with sister gray wolf,
Where the desert sage brush grows.
Heal me, open me,
Release my true heart song,

Transform the shadows in my soul
Into gifts of peace and love.

I am a medicine woman,
I seek the healing way;
Reveal the vision in my heart
For wisdom, this I pray.

Heal me, open me,
Release my true heart song;
Let my vision heal the world
My whole life long.

8. When the mood is right, *all the women link hands and begin danc-ing and singing* until an ululation rises from their throats. The group then breaks bread, shares food, and eventually makes their way home.

11
Rosh Hodesh: Celebration of the New Moon

SHEKINAH IS "Lady of the Moon," keeper of the calendars of cycles. Shekinah carries the ancient connections between women's menstrual cycle, the cycles of the moon, and the cycles of the tides, connections that are evident in ancient iconography.

A BRIEF HISTORY

The religion of ancient peoples was expressed in relationship to the cycles of life and death, of women's fertility, of agriculture and the seasons, and of the heavens. Ancient art celebrates the feminine aspect of these cycles with specific iconography, the construction of sacred shrines, and in the creation of holy days. The natural day of rest in a lunar cycle is the new moon, the first day of the new monthly cycle. Cultures worldwide feature New Moon ceremonies. Among the ancient Israelites, this day was called Rosh Hodesh: *Rosh* means "head of," and *Hodesh*, derived from the Hebrew root that means "to make new," means "month." At one time Rosh Hodesh and the Sabbath were celebrated with equal importance. Both were times when people performed no work and gathered to eat a special meal and offer prayers. Trumpets were blown to announce the onset of the holy day.

But Rosh Hodesh's mythology was tied to the worship of goddesses, the use of fertility figures, to women's proclamation of oracles, and to the honoring of women's fertility cycles. Rosh Hodesh did not develop a "Jewish mythology" until more than seven hundred years after the Bible was canonized. According to *Pirke Eliezer,* a rabbinic midrash compiled in the eighth century, the women of Israel refused to donate any gold for the purpose of making the golden calf. As a reward for their faithfulness, God gave the women Rosh Hodesh. The story is meant to explain why women consider Rosh Hodesh their holy day.

By the second century C.E., Rosh Hodesh had been relegated to a minor holy day as men widened the scope of their authority to include the determination of calendar days and the leadership of public ritual. But women maintained their connection to the most ancient of holy days by preserving the ritual acts associated with that day, and with Shabbat: the baking of special bread, the lighting of fire, and the cessation of work.

Still, the origin of these acts in women's religion is not known to most Jewish women, and the midrashic explanations for them are cast in negative stereotypes about women. As an explanation for why women remove a piece of dough from the Sabbath bread and burn it in the oven, a midrash says: Adam was God's bread offering to the world and Eve defiled it. As expiation for their sin, all women are commanded to separate a "heave offering" from the dough. As an explanation for why women light holy day candles, another midrash contends: Women extinguish the light of man's soul, therefore she is bidden to kindle the Sabbath light. And menstruation is viewed as a source of ritual defilement for men. Menstruating women are still taboo to strict Orthodox men.

The three women's mitzrot in Judaism—challah, family purity laws, which regulate menstruation, and lighting candles—are said to have originated in sin and are expiatory rituals. Yet the true origins of these rituals lie in customs from cultures that honored women and upheld their importance in the community. If we are to revive the positive associations for women of bread, moon, and blood, we must recover the authentic origins of these rituals.

All three of these ritual acts are tied to women's practices around the lunar and menstrual cycle. Baking bread on a holy day, for instance, is an ancient custom tied to Goddess worship around the world. In the ancient Near East women baked bread to Asherah, forming the cakes in Her image.

The Eastern European custom of braiding the challah derives from the practice of braiding bread to resemble the hair of Berches, the Goddess of the Hearth. Because Sabbath is called Queen and Bride, Jewish women were able to adapt the folk custom for their own use. In addition, the word *challah* appears to be related to the word for women's dancing called *mahol* and refers to round dancing and holding bread while dancing and praying. Women baked cakes to the Goddess on the new moon as a way of celebrating the renewal of the substance of life and to give expression to her Presence through the bread.

When the tribes relied only on lunar calendars, the Sabbath, every seventh day, most likely fell on the new moon, the waxing moon, the full moon, or the waning moon—that is, on the first, seventh, fourteenth, or twenty-first day of the lunar cycle. The entire ceremonial calendar also seems to have been tied to women's menstrual cycles.

Niddah, or menstruation, is also related to the New Moon and to the Sabbath. The word *Sabbath,* or *sabbatu,* refers to the rest of the Goddess during her menses! Sabbatu, or a day of rest, most likely originated around women's menstrual cycle as a time when women congregated and sought vision. Rosh Hodesh was once a time when men and women visited holy shrines to consult with oracle women to receive direction for the coming moon. To this day, women often experience a higher amount of psychic awareness during their flow.

It is common knowledge, and a researched fact, that women who live together in close quarters tend to bleed concurrently. A mikveh lady who worked in New York confirmed this to me. She testified that most of the Orthodox women used the mikveh during the new and the full moon. It was further confirmed by my own experience on the occasion of the second Rosh Hodesh I celebrated with the women in Philadelphia, a month after the first. We met at Suri Lebow's house in the country. Penina lay on the floor moaning about menstrual cramps. Suri joined in, so did Andy and I, and then several other women also noted they were having their periods. We were amazed. Even though we weren't living together in the same house, the spiritual impact of the last Rosh Hodesh had somehow brought us into synchronicity. It was the moon of Shevat, when we celebrate the rising of the sap in the trees. We all went outside and sat under Suri's enormous beech tree, joined hands, and meditated on the connection between menstruation, moon, and our holy day.

Since that time, hundreds of Jewish women have returned to the practice of Rosh Hodesh as a time to explore feminism and Judaism. I would like to offer a ceremony that can serve as a model for ceremonies throughout the year and that can create a time and place for women to explore sources of Jewish women's spirituality.

GUIDELINES FOR A ROSH HODESH CEREMONY

Rosh Hodesh, like Shabbat and all our days, begins at sundown. Arrange your time so you can tie up loose ends at work in order to celebrate the holy day. Traditional women took one or two days off from doing housework, as Rosh Hodesh is sometimes one or two days long. The lunar calendar was eventually synchronized with the solar calendar for the purpose of planting and harvesting. Thus the lunar calendar is based on a nineteen-year cycle in which years alternate in a fixed manner between twelve and thirteen months. Look to the skies and you will know when the new moon occurs. It is a sliver of light that appears at twilight close to the western horizon.

Prepare the space you are going to use in the same way you would decorate for a Mishkan ceremony. For the first time, I suggest a place with a sauna, hot tub, or steam room (unless natural springs are available). You will need to bring special breads and cakes, candles, and objects which represent the theme of the month you are celebrating.

The Order of Service

1. The women gather around the altar in a circle and one woman begins to lead a song and dance. The simplest dance is stepping sideways with the left foot and moving your right foot next to it. Keep moving clockwise. Dance one full circle around the altar and come back to your original place. Sing something you know and feel comfortable with. A wordless melody often works best.

2. The fires of Rosh Hodesh are lit and one woman reads the following:

Prayer for Lighting the Fires of the New Moon

We are keepers of the flame, Eshet lapidot.
Like Devorah, we make the wicks for the Mishkan's
  eternal light
And kindle the fires of holy time.
Fire transmutes substance,
Grain into bread,
Clay into pot,
Cold into the warmth of the hearth.
With this flame we honor Shekinah,
Mother and Creator,
And we initiate this holy day, Rosh Hodesh.
Brucha Yah Shekinah ha-m'kadeshet o-tanu
u'm'hadeshet o-tanu al yadei hadlakat ner shel
  Rosh Hodesh.

> *Blessed is Yah Shekinah, who consecrates us and*
>
>   *renews us*
>
> *through the lighting of the fires of Rosh Hodesh.*

3. The women join in a song for the month. The months and themes of Rosh Hodesh are as follows.

Tevet, Moon of returning light. Rosh Hodesh Tevet is the seventh day of Hanukkah (which occurs around the winter solstice) and is celebrated as the day to remember Judith, the heroine who beheaded the wicked Holofernes. We tell the stories about the descent of heroines to the underworld in search of new wisdom.

Shevat, Moon of the sap rising in the trees. During Shevat we celebrate the new year of the trees, and the tree as a symbol of our people. As the sap rises and the light returns, we tell stories of pioneer women who blossomed early and cleared paths for us to follow.

Adar, the Moon of Queen Esther. Adar is sometimes celebrated twice as the twelfth and thirteenth moon. Adar is the time we celebrate the story of Queen Esther, who revealed her true identity to the king in order to save her people. We remember Persian and other Middle Eastern women's traditions with belly dancing, drumming, and feasting, and we tell stories about women who saved lives.

Nisan, Liberation Moon. This is the season of our freedom. We remember the women of the exodus generation and tell stories about women who struggle for justice.

Iyar, Journey Moon. We tell the story of our wanderings in the wilderness in search of the proverbial promised land, and how we healed ourselves from old wounds to make ready for new revelations.

Sivan, Moon of revelations. Sivan is the month we received the Torah on Mount Sinai, both the written and oral tradition. During Sivan we share Torat HaShekinah, Torah wisdom from women in Jewish tradition.

Tammuz, Moon of premonitions. This is the moon when the first brick in the wall protecting the Temple in Jerusalem is removed from its foundation, which was the first step toward its destruction. We tell stories about someone's premonitions as a source of wisdom.

Av, Moon of the vine dance. Av is the moon when wealthier women exchanged white garments with poor women so the very poor would be dressed in the garments of the rich. The women went out into the fields to dance among the grapevines, calling upon and renewing the beauty within. We tell stories of women who walk in beauty even in times of trouble.

Elul, Moon of "I am to my beloved as my beloved is to me." We prepare ourselves for the new year of the soul by creating amulets that bear the sign of protection and strength for us. Then we learn to blow the shofar!

Tishri, Moon of balances. This is the national holy day of all the people. Women can celebrate Rosh Hodesh on the evening of the second day, if there is the opportunity to do so. We go to the shvitz and sweat for the new year to purify our feminine nature.

Heshvan, Flood Moon. We celebrate the yarzeit (death anniversary) of Rachel and tell flood tales. We meditate on the meaning of water in our lives and learn to use a mikveh.

Kislev, Moon of rededication. The time we reconsecrate our life to the keeping of the ways of our people even as we invest old symbols with new meaning. We tell stories of women who helped us stay connected to our culture.

4. We name ourselves through as many generations as we can go back on the mother's side, or we name ourselves by a spiritual attribute called upon for the occasion.

The second way of naming can be a chant composed on the spot. It is an improvisational prayer of women's names. Someone shakes a rattle and begins: "We think of an attribute or aspect of our lives and we name ourselves as such":

> *Writing a book woman*
> *Walks with courage woman*
> *Must learn to say no woman*
> *Grandmother of four boys woman*

and so forth. The chant weaves together a wonderful tapestry of our lives.

5. We engage in the specific activity designated by the women gathered. Use the themes listed in number 3 as a guide. Pass a talking stick if you are sharing stories. When a person is done speaking, she may say, "May Shekinah be with you." The congregation responds, "And may Shekinah be with you."

6. We stand and pass a bowl of waters to anoint and bless each other for the coming month. Spontaneous prayers are said to the woman on our right-hand side.

7. We dance and sing closing songs. Check the bibliography for sources.

8. We say a blessing over the fruit of the vine and give thanks for the holy day of Rosh Hodesh. Find a melody that comes from women's sources for this blessing as you dance a grapevine pattern. If you don't know how to dance a grapevine, find out from a friend.

9. *We break the bread.* The community names women whose bread they loved. Here is one way to introduce this activity:

The Naming of Bread-Baking Women

This round loaf feeds the people we love.
Let us recount women who baked bread
And from whom we learned our recipe.

Shekinah, Bread of Our Souls

Shekinah, like bread,
Is manna to our souls.
She feeds us the yeast
That helps us rise to the occasion.
Brucha Yah Shekinah hamotziah lechem min ha adamah.
Blessed is Shekinah who brings forth the bread.

10. We eat, schmooze, and eventually go home . . . unless we're on a retreat!

Almost two decades ago I was reminded of women's universal and ancient relationship to bread, blood, fire, and moon. In a show of support for women's right to choose, women of many ethnic groups gathered in ceremony opposite the White House, in Lafayette Park. Each of us brought bread representing our particular ethnic identity. We created an altar piled high with indigenous breads: rice cakes, tortillas, challahs, fry breads, and corn breads—all shapes and sizes. We lit a fire, encircled the bread, and sang to the music of Sweet Honey in the Rock. Strength emanated from the circle. There was sisterhood in the bread, in the fire, in our bodies, in our support of the right to choose how and when to bear a child, and in our awareness of our ability to transform and to nourish and to create community. May Shekinah be with you.

12
Ceremonies for Women's Lives

INITIATION OF THE NEW JEWISH WOMAN

THE INITIATION of children into adulthood, the Bar Mitzvah, is one of the most important rituals in our tradition. Until recently this coming of age ritual was available only to boys, since the occasion entailed reading the Torah from the pulpit in the synagogue, an activity prohibited to women.

Since Judith Kaplan was called to the Torah in honor of her Bat Mitzvah by her father Mordecai Kaplan seventy-five years ago, a growing trend has developed to mark a girl's passage into womanhood with ceremony. Over the last twenty years I have developed a four-part initiation for girls that includes a preparation period of eight months, a vision quest in the mountains, an initiation into Rosh Hodesh, and a Saturday morning Bat Mitzvah prayer service. Boys undergo a similar experience, without the Rosh Hodesh ceremony.

Preparation

At my congregation in Albuquerque, Nahalat Shalom (Inheritance of Peace), preparation for Bat Mitzvah is a tremendous commitment of time and energy on the part of a young woman. Bat Mitzvah requires learning more than twenty-five Hebrew songs, reading forty different prayers in Hebrew, chanting from the Torah, preparing a speech or some other kind of presentation, learning to play the *beladi* rhythm on the drum, learning a prayer in sign language, and developing a style of presentation.

The successful outcome of the Bat Mitzvah depends on the child's relationship with the teacher. The size of my congregation still permits me the opportunity to try to develop a loving relationship with all the children from the time they are born or enter the congregation. Getting to know them over time eases the tensions inherent in the Bar and Bat Mitzvah experience. As the teacher who prepares them forty-five minutes a week for six to eight months,

- I assist them as they work through their decision to commit themselves to the service;

- I confront the need for discipline as I help them establish a style and rhythm of study and practice;

- I convey the importance of honesty in the teacher-student relationship (some students try to trick me about how much they've practiced and are surprised that I know when they haven't);

- I help them to develop their own opinions and ideas about Judaism and, using the Bat Mitzvah, to create an original body of work that expresses their unique perspectives on a concern raised by their Torah study;

- I nurture the communication between parent and child and find ways to enrich the Jewish experience of the parents through their child's Bar or Bat Mitzvah;

- I let the students know each time what a wonderful job they are doing and how much they are loved, and I use a lot of humor.

Vision Quest

In the summer just before or after their Bat Mitzvah ceremony, a group of girls is taken into the mountains of New Mexico (we have several preferred sites) for a camping experience we call vision quest. The Bat Mitzvah is meant to give young people a high degree of self-confidence, which comes from successfully meeting a difficult challenge. If this self-confidence can also come through Jewish experiences, I believe children will stay rooted in their culture, because the culture fostered their growth in a positive way. Vision quest is yet another challenge.

GUIDELINES

Find a beautiful and secluded location. The woman leading the group should have a lot of experience camping, which includes knowing about first aid and water purification and having a sense of what is physically possible to accomplish on this trip. This is not meant to be a serious physical challenge in the wilderness; it's simply an invigorating adventure that includes a two- to four-mile round trip hike to the vision quest location from the campsite.

The girls are responsible for camping tasks, which are worked out ahead of time so that set up and break down and cooking run smoothly. Keep it simple.

The order of events is as follows:

1. Arrive and set up camp toward the late afternoon. Preparing dinner and lighting the campfire are the main evening activities of the first night. The girls will have brought a good selection of Jewish women's stories, myths, fairy tales, and riddles to tell or read centered on the theme of growing up.

2. Go to sleep at a reasonable hour so you can wake up at daybreak.

3. If you are camping near a waterfall or hot springs, the morning can begin (after someone makes the fire) with a mikveh. Most girls will want to wear bathing suits, as teens are extremely shy about unveiling in public.

4. After breakfast begin the vision quest. I tell them about the title Eshet Hazon, "Woman of Vision," which my friend Hannah Siegel was given by Jewish communities in the Pacific Northwest in recognition of

her spiritual leadership. I remind them that women have been honored as seers from the time of Miriam the prophet onward. I tell them how important it is for us as women to develop the craft of imagination to guide us through life, so we can be creative problem solvers and managers of our many responsibilities. And we need our imagination along with our ability to endure through the hard times in order to realize our dreams.

5. Pack up water and lunch and set out in silence with the intention of using the silence to become deeply aware of all that is around you. It is helpful if children are taken out at a younger age and initiated into the art of silence in the vision quest so that this is not a first-time experience.

6. When you arrive at the intended site (a mountain crest with a view works well), sit down and have one of the older girls begin to shake a rattle. She will have written a prayerful intention for the occasion, which she recites. It might be something like, "What we seek today are signs of our inner strength. As we sit with eyes open or closed, let us become empty. Let us become a Mishkan for our vision. Let us be open to what feeds our spirit and invests us with compassionate strength. Go now and find a place on the mountain and make a dwelling place for Shekinah."

7. After about twenty to thirty minutes, one of the girls blows a shofar, and everyone returns to the meeting place. Each girl is given a little pad and pencil to record some of what they have experienced. Then join hands and sing a closing song that the girls have chosen for this part of the ceremony. After this, break bread and eat.

8. The hike back down the mountain is more playful, as is the rest of the afternoon.

9. Toward evening build a campfire and share your mountaintop visions. Pass a talking stick and allow each girl to talk about what she views as her inner strengths.

10. Sing another song chosen by the girls, drink some ceremonial fruit of the vine, break bread, and throw some canned beans into a pot. After a meal of beans and tortillas, we roast the kosher marshmallows, tell more stories, sing more songs, and drum late into the night.

11. As you head out the next day, you may wish to visit a tourist spot or some other site of interest, or you may simply drive straight home.

The vision quest experience can be turned into a painting, a dance, a short story, a poem, or a musical composition to be shared at a later date as a part of the congregation's holy day liturgy.

Rosh Hodesh Initiation

An experience unique to women is, of course, the onset of menses. It is the physical sign of one's approaching womanhood. Although Jewish tradition emphasizes the spiritual and intellectual passage over the physical, the bodily changes that begin at about the age of twelve nonetheless deserve attention. Girls are fascinated by the topic of "getting" their period. Once while I was visiting friends in North Carolina, a ten-year-old girl named Maren wanted to hear every detail of the menses ritual I had just conducted in New York. She kept begging me for more stories—"What happened to her?" When I finally exhausted my supply of stories, she asked for repeats, and we sat for another hour going over the tales I had just shared.

Initiating Jewish girls into the covenant of the New Moon around the time of their Bat Mitzvah and menses gives us an opportunity to pass on our women's wisdom, to promote their self-esteem and their sense of dignity, which young women need from their communities to help them make good choices and to give them the courage to protect, honor, and listen to their body's voices. We need to teach our daughters how to walk the streets in such a way that they can avoid violence. We need to encourage them to use their wits for safety, when to say yes and no, and how to seek help if they need it. Rosh Hodesh celebrations can establish the caring circle that holds, protects, encourages, nurtures, and sends forth women into the world.

GUIDELINES

I usually spend one session with the girls in preparation for this ceremony. Each writes a blessing that honors seven aspects of herself that she values.

I have found the moon of Elul to be appropriate for this occasion, because it occurs just before school starts and it helps the girls bond again before the start of the season.

One special feature of this ceremony is the color red. Everyone wears red garments, and we use red flowers, cloth, and foods to decorate the space. The color symbolizes life and blood.

This ceremony was designed with Rebecca Narva, who wanted to bring her daughter into the circle.

1. The girls are led into the center of the Rosh Hodesh circle. They pass under a red huppah held on four poles and are showered with rose petals and songs as they enter. Their mothers accompany them through the huppah. They sit on red pillows in the center of the circle underneath the huppah. One woman says, "The huppah is a garment suspended on four poles usually used at a wedding. It harks back to the Mishkan of the wilderness period and so symbolizes the sanctuary of the Shekinah. Tonight we hold up the red huppah of your womanhood."

2. The women greet the girls:

"Henai mah tov u-mah nayim shevet nashim gam yachad.

How good and how pleasant, women sitting together in kinship."

3. The eldest woman lights the Rosh Hodesh candles and pronounces a blessing.

4. Each participant celebrates the chain of tradition by reciting her own Hebrew or Yiddish or Spanish name and then naming the women from her mother's side as many generations back as possible.

5. We sing a song in honor of Shekinah:

"We all come from Shekinah, and to her we will return

Like a drop of water flowing to the ocean."

6. Each of the mothers will have created a bead necklace or amulet for her daughter. Amulets made by women enjoy a long history in Jewish women's culture. They are signs of protection used around significant life occasions. (These can be made, for instance, from pieces from charm bracelets, beads collected over time, or paper beads that mother and daughter make themselves. Amulets can be made from clay [fimo works well] or copper purchased at a craft store.) Place the necklaces in a basket and pass it around the circle. The basket honors women's invention of basketry and storage vessels. We are weavers of experience and storers of wisdom. Each woman holds the basket and tells what it was

like the first time she menstruated. She then shares a blessing and a piece of wisdom that she wants to transmit to the girls.

7. The mothers place the necklaces around their daughters and bestow a special blessing on them that they have composed.

8. The daughters recite a blessing for themselves that they compose with their rabbi, mother, or teacher. The formula is: "I bless my _____." Each girl has been asked to think of seven aspects of herself that she honors in herself. For instance, "I bless my athletic ability, my ability to make friends, my interest in music . . ."

9. Then the women lead the antiphonal "Blessing for Becoming a Woman." The girls repeat each verse in the first person.

Blessing for Becoming a Woman

Eshet hayil you are,

Eshet hayil I am,

A woman of your people.

A woman of my people.

Upon the heart courage path you walk.

Upon the heart courage path I walk.

You follow your way through the wilderness.

I follow my way through the wilderness.

You greet your spirit strength,

I greet my spirit strength,

And she guides you.

And she guides me.

Up the mountain you go,

Up the mountain I go,

With courage you ascend.

With courage I ascend.

You have no fear of rising to the heights.

I have no fear of rising to the heights.
You are a daughter of your people.
I am a daughter of my people.
Eshet hayil you are.
Eshet hayil I am.
On the justice path you walk.
On the justice path I walk.
To the depths you descend,
To the depths I descend,
Seeking the wisdom of women.
Seeking the wisdom of women.
You move with grace below
I move with grace below
To reveal the truth living in the depths of your heart.
To reveal the truth living in the depths of my heart.
You forge a path in the Abyss.
I forge a path in the Abyss.
Your wisdom you vow to cherish.
My wisdom I vow to cherish.
Your special gifts you vow to honor.
My special gifts I vow to honor.
Your body you vow to love.
My body I vow to love.
This night you receive your womanhood
By the dark of the new moon.
You choose to enter the covenant of your sisters
And celebrate Rosh Hodesh.
May you be blessed with _____

[the women call out one- or two-word blessings].
May you be blessed with peace.

Now the girls are lifted up in chairs and the women dance and sing around them to welcome them into the covenant of the New Moon. This is followed by the blessings of wine and bread and a festive meal. Strawberries dipped in chocolate are a favorite for this occasion.

Bar and Bat Mitzvah

Bar and Bat Mitzvah can be a wonderful experience in the life of a young person and her family. Many families invite, in addition to local guests, out-of-town relatives and friends (sometimes fifty or more!), who often travel great distances to attend the ceremony. The excitement can be overwhelming.

At Nahalat Shalom we begin the formal festivities with a Kabbalat Shabbat for friends and family. The Bat Mitzvah, her grandmother, her mother's and father's sister(s), and her mother come up to light candles together. She also stands with her grandfather, her father's and mother's brother(s), and her father to recite the kiddush. All the children are called to hold up the braided challah, which is traditionally served on Friday nights, and everyone recites the blessing. We tear the bread with our hands and pass it.

After dinner the family and community gather for a brief service of Jewish women's poetry and liturgy, along with some traditional prayers.

Instead of a sermon during the service, family members tell stories about relatives and forebears the children may not know. The Bat Mitzvah serves as a time to pass on family histories. You may want to present a calligraphied family tree to the Bat Mitzvah on this occasion.

The morning is devoted to the traditional service. The Bat Mitzvah leads the Hebrew sections of the service, and the congregation chants in English.

I have chosen to train children to read extensively from the Torah in place of learning a Haftorah. The Haftorah is not chanted from a scroll,

as is the Torah, and so is less impressive for the children. For them
chanting from the Torah itself is the most meaningful aspect of the service. After the Torah is taken out of the ark and paraded around the congregation, the whole assembly is invited to the pulpit to see the unrolled
Torah. As people file by, I give a brief history of our Torah and answer
questions about how it was made, where it comes from, and so forth.

After the Bat Mitzvah chants from the Torah, she presents her speech.
We encourage the children at Nahalat Shalom to be creative in the arts
by giving them a ceremonial role at every major holy day. The speech,
therefore, is perhaps the centerpiece of their initiation. It is the time they
unfold their ideas through an artistic medium. I would like to recount
one particular girl's choice of presentation.

At her Rosh Hodesh initiation, which had occurred several months
before her Bat Mitzvah, Gwen Fletcher approached me with a question.
"Rabbi Lynn, do you think my Bat Mitzvah could be funny?"

"Funny? As in stand-up comedy and jokes?"

Gwen's eyes twinkled. "Yeah . . ." I saw her mother roll her eyes. Gwen
had seen me perform many times, and she had been in many dramatic
presentations at Nahalat Shalom. Her Torah portion dealt with a long
list of curses that would befall the Israelites if they strayed from God's
commandments. A comic approach to the material was her way of getting a handle on the text. It was a brilliant solution.

"Sure, that sounds like a good direction," I said. "What did you have
in mind?"

Her mother, shaking her head in disbelief, uttered, "Comedy? What
will the relatives think?"

I explained that comedy is a solemn tradition among the Jews. I told
her the Talmudic story of a rabbi who accompanies Elijah to the mar-
ketplace and wants to know who is going to paradise. Elijah points out
two jesters and says, "These two, because they make people laugh."

Gwen's mother smiled and lightened up. "Well, Rabbi Lynn, I guess I
trust you."

Gwen and I plotted a course. She checked out several books from the
library that dealt with Jewish humor and selected several of her favorite

jokes. She read an article in the *Big Book of Jewish Humor* that gave a historical perspective to her studies. Then she created an old woman she called Zetch the Kvetch. Zetch was supposed to be Gwen's grandmother "to the tenth degree." She lived as a girl during the time of the exodus from Egypt and was going to describe her experience of leaving Egypt. Gwen made a mask, designed a costume for Zetch, and wrote a twenty-minute monologue. This was a student whose voice was barely audible when she recited her prayers! I would stand in my kitchen boiling tea and ask her to shout to me from the living room. After months of work, she raised her voice above a whisper. But when she put on Zetch's mask, Gwen became another person. She was truly funny. Her relatives and friends from the congregation were captivated and amazed by her humor and poise. Zetch was both profound and funny and she shed new light on her Torah portion. Gwen continues to develop her comic talents in school and in the congregation.

Children at Nahalat Shalom benefit from a creative approach to this all-important ceremony. And they all love the parties thrown in their honor. The party is payback for all the months of hard work and sacrifice they undertook to show their loyalty to their culture. They deserve good food, good music, and a great time.

One final note about the expense of the ceremony. Jewish tradition does not encourage lavishness to the point of overindulgence at ceremonies. In a time when so many people both worldwide and in our own communities suffer the indignities of poverty, it is better to spend less and donate a considerable amount of money to a charity chosen by the Bar or Bat Mitzvah and his or her parents. Those attending the Bat Mitzvah or Bar Mitzvah ceremony might also be asked to bring food for donation to a women's shelter or a local food bank.

A MOTHER'S DAILY PRAYER

With all the emphasis on the importance of motherhood in Jewish tradition it is rather surprising to find so little in the way of liturgy that addresses mothering. Married women (who are presumed to have children) are honored on the eve of the Sabbath with the recitation of

Proverbs 31:10–31, known as *eshet hayil*, "the woman of valor," and the entire Song of Songs. Eshet hayil appears to be advice given to a certain King Lemuel by his mother on the qualities he should look for in a wife. She should be a woman who rises before dawn, works industriously all day, is kind and discreet, knows how to spin and sew, manages her household, and does business with her wares. She should be a credit to her husband and her children. How she should care for her children is not of concern. In the Song of Songs a young woman whose strong, defiant voice is the heart of the text speaks of her desire to bring her beloved to her mother's house and make love to him in the "bed of the one who conceived me." We get the impression that the mother not only approves but has even instructed her daughter in the art of intimacy. But her mother's voice never surfaces to confirm our suspicion.

Since the late sixteenth century there has existed a body of prayers collected in women's prayer books known in Yiddish as *Tkhinnes,* or "supplicatory prayers." Although several prominent women wrote in this genre, these prayers were composed mostly by men for women. Nonetheless their immense popularity points to the need for liturgy that addresses women's unique concerns. The subject matter of Tkhinnes covers a variety of occasions, including prayers for the new moon, for lighting Sabbath candles, for removing the tip of the Sabbath bread, for childbirth, to prevent miscarriage, for leading a child to heder for the first time, and for one's husband as he sets out on a business trip. Although Tkhinnes are a fascinating window into the lives of Eastern European women, they are not an adequate source of prayer for contemporary Jewish women. Our standards of piety and mothering have changed. More important, we need prayers that reflect our own voices.

Other sources for mother prayers are the folk songs of the Jewish world, stretching from India to the Middle East, Africa, Europe, and the Americas. Often the themes of folk music address women's concerns directly because women composed and sang it. Most of the music is about romantic love between men and women, not the trials and joys of mothering. We do possess lullabies, however, and here we finally come closest to mothers' liturgy, employed when we try to put our children to sleep so that we might enjoy some quiet time at the end of the day.

The following prayer is the result of much consultation with mother friends, whose children range from infant to adolescent, the span that actively engages us in our children's daily lives. Everyone expressed excitement about reading a daily mothering prayer and added their own set of supplicatory needs. This prayer is not attached to a special occasion; rather it is meant to be used whenever mothers need to turn to She Who Mothers Creation for strength and love to sustain us from moment to moment as we rear our children.

↞ *A Mother's Daily Prayer*

Wild Mother of earth and sky,
You who nestle seed in clay
And lift up winged creatures on Your wind,
Enliven me with morning grace
As I awake to mothering.

If I have time to say these words
And You have time to listen,
Keep my children safe from harm,
Bless them with healthy bodies and minds.
Let them flourish.

Winsome Mother of sea and stream,
You who move it all along,
Grant me humor, patience, and compassion
To flow with the day that beckons me now
To fix breakfast, check homework, and answer the phone.

Cosmic Mother of stars and destiny,
Who juggles time and child,
If I have not yet been interrupted
I pray also for these things:

[Add your personal prayers]

Wise Mother who gives and takes away,
Who sets the boundaries of work and play,
May we all love and forgive each other
Yet another day.
And grant me the stillness of quiet hours
To renew and refresh my mothering.
Amen.

GROWING OLDER

"How are you?" I asked Sarah Sorenson, may her memory be a blessing, as she munched a piece of Alice Hiat's delicious Shabbos chicken. At 101 years of age, Sarah was still swimming every day, was as radical as ever, and peppered every comment with her wit.

"It still tastes good," responded Sarah, commenting on the chicken and life in general. Sarah comes to mind when I think of elder women I want to emulate as I approach fifty. I wish there were more formal ways to honor my elders. Rituals and storytelling can frame the movement of our lives and provide occasions to reflect upon, share, and give value to our life experiences. Women's lives have certainly lacked the formal marking of passages, but both men and women suffer from an absence of rituals for the later years. It is this gap in ceremony that I will address here.

With improved health care and natural hardiness, growing older can last quite a long time, sometimes several decades. It is fitting, therefore, that rituals honoring elders be divided into at least two categories: women entering their fifties and sixties and women crossing into their seventies, eighties, and nineties. Both ceremonies offered here can be adapted to the lives of men.

The first stage of growing older can be a time of great freedom and productivity for women. At this age we are past the daily child-rearing and householding tasks and have more uninterrupted hours to devote to creative pursuits. For other women years of work experience in public or artistic careers may be flowering into full recognition and financial and emotional rewards at this stage of life. A ritual for "young crones," which I have titled "The Fruits of Creation," can support women as they actively explore and embrace new interests and can honor them for their achievements thus far.

The second stage of aging produces a desire to sum up our lives, a kind of putting one's house in order. Elders appreciate having a public forum in which to remember and to be heard. I call the ritual for aged women "Honoring the Years." The intergenerational dimension of the last ritual for a living elder is especially important.

Fruits of Creation Ceremony

A woman may choose to observe this rite of passage to mark any number of life transitions: children leaving home, the onset of menopause, recovery from a midlife illness such as breast cancer, a midlife divorce, the start of a new career path, or simply entry into a new decade. The following ceremony is told as a story and is based on a ritual designed by a woman I shall call Zahavah: Goldenwoman. She had just turned fifty, left her husband, sent a son off to college, and begun a new job! The women of Rosh Hodesh usually serve as the congregation for women's passages. We are like the ever-present chorus of female voices found in the Bible in the Song of Songs, the Book of Ruth, Lamentations, the story of Jephthah's daughter, and on other occasions when women gathered with their collective poetry and dance. I have divided both rituals into stages, which I have numbered and named.

1. To the woods

The Rosh Hodesh Circle of Nahalat Shalom prefers to make ceremony in the midst of piñon-covered mountains, where no walls or ceilings limit the flight of our spirit. Earth, sky, water, and fire become Shekinah's Temple. We sit on her holy red mud, breathe in the scent of pine, submerge in her water holes, and kindle a tiny fire.

One predawn morning in February we head to the Jemez Mountains and follow a trail that leads to hot springs. A deer crosses our path. We disrobe in the chilly morning under a moon on the western horizon.

2. Mikveh meditation

As we ease into the water, Zahavah leads us in a meditation to guide us inward.

Old Woman of Wisdom Meditation

Imagine yourself
Old woman,
Hair silver as the fading moon,
Skin wrinkled and worn thin,
Bones stiff as winter wheat in a snowy field.
But life still tastes good
Above and below.
Imagine yourself
Old woman
Brimming with wisdom's light,
Knowing, as you do, ebb and flow,
Having seen death wash up on your shore,
Carried home parts of it in your pocket,
Arranged it on your altar and said prayers.
Old woman,
Your belly shaking with laughter,
Savoring the miracle of every hour,
Let this water heal and replenish
The spirit within you.
Flowing,

Let this mikveh bless and sanctify
The wellspring of wisdom
That sets you free.

We submerge twice in the fetal position and Zahavah says:

✍ *A Blessing*

Blessed are you, Shekinah,
Wise Elder, Ancient Mother,
Who renews and sanctifies us
With the waters of this mikveh.

3. Creating an Altar

We dress and move closer to the entrance of a nearby cave. We place objects we have brought on a bed of pine needles, which we encircle with stones. Some of the objects include a picture of someone's grandmother, a seashell representing the ability to hear the earth speak, a clay oil-burning lamp, a lace doily from a great-aunt, a book of Adrienne Rich's poems, a small sculpture of spider woman, a mirror, a safety pin representing our ability to hold things together. All are aspects of women's wisdom. When we finish arranging the objects, we light the oil lamp, burn some juniper, and Zahavah says a blessing.

4. Headdress Totafot

"And you shall bind them as a sign upon your head."

It has become a custom among the women who celebrate Rosh Hodesh in Albuquerque to weave a wreath of flowers or design a clay or silk headdress for the woman we honor as young crone. We derive this custom from ancient times, when women priestesses in the Middle East wore *totafot* on their third eye. Totafot are not described in the Bible but are depicted on statues of priestesses and goddesses looking out the windows of seven-pillared shrines. These sacred headdresses are the prototypes for *tefillin*, small black leather boxes containing scrolls upon which are written the Shema and its blessing. Tefillin are donned by Orthodox men as part of the morning weekday prayer. Hannah Siegel, a woman ordained as an *Eshet Hazon* (Woman of Vision) by alternative Jews living in the Pacific Northwest, designed cloth tefillin for her community as well. Many women replace the traditional quotation found in the tefillin with words from women's wisdom lore. When we place the totafot on Zahavah's head, we read a passage adapted from the Book of Proverbs that describes the divine personification of Wisdom known as Hochma.

✧ *A Reading of Wisdom's Instruction*

Wisdom built her shrine,

Hewed seven pillars,

Prepared a feast, and set her table.

She sent forth her priestesses

To summits of rolling hills

To cross roads and city gates.

She calls the inhabitants to her place:

"Listen to the words I speak.

Truth is upon my lips.

Righteousness is in my heart.

I am Wisdom everlasting.

Say to me, You are my sister.

Seek my instruction and you shall live."

5. *Designing the breastplate*

The breastplate is yet another garment of power taken away from priestesses and given to priests. The breastplate was worn by women who interpreted oracles (the name Devorah can mean "Oracle Woman") and is one of seven sacred garments Inanna wears in her descent to the under-

world. Zahavah wanted to fashion a breastplate as part of her crone ceremony. We designed a Jewish woman's *ephod* (the Hebrew name for
breastplate) and asked each woman present to paint a symbol of
women's wisdom on the plate. Zahavah leads us in another meditation
to help us access the images. A rattle or shaker is used to help us go
within.

Zahava says:

> *Return to the waters of the mikveh*
> *and explore the images of our wisdom that greet us*
>   *in the depths.*
> *The tokens of your wisdom are gifts from Shekinah;*
> *She sets them upon the altar,*
> *She instructs you in their use,*
> *She guides you to see them with your inner eye.*
> *We sing to them.*

The rattle continues and we begin to chant through our breath.
Slowly we weave the strands of melody together to create a song among
us. The song comes to its conclusion through an intuitive process. We
end together.

Each of us is given a shape cut from paper or cloth that belongs to the
breastplate and some begin to paint the token of their wisdom shield.
When we finish, we glue our section onto the shield. Some of us have
strung beads, which we attach to the bottom of the shield. We share the
meaning of our token, and after all have spoken, we place the ephod on
Zahavah with the following blessing:

The Blessing of the Breastplate

> *We consecrate this shield*
> *in the name of Shekinah.*
> *May this shield*

be a sign and a memory

in your coming and going

that Shekinah is with you.

She spreads her wings over you

and blesses you with peace.

Zahavah Eshet Hochma, Em Yisrael,

May your wisdom be a blessing upon us

and upon your people.

6. Reading from Ruth

I suggest that the reading of the Book of Ruth be included as an element in both aging ceremonies. At a time when the company of other women grows increasingly important for women, this story affirms women in their relationships. It is the only story in the Bible that celebrates women's support of one another. Ruth, which means "friendship," breaks all the normal conventions of biblical tales. God in this story does not reveal Himself from a bush or a mountain or in a dream or direct speech. Rather the presence of God is manifest through the love and caring of one woman for another. The text raises up the most marginalized of women, a Moabite widow without children or land, as a model for the overcoming of suffering through the act of devotion to another marginalized human being. In many folk narratives the relationship between mother-in-law and wife is often fraught with friction and tension. In this story Ruth's devoted love for Naomi redeems them both. Instead of competing for one man's love, they share this love and make it work for them both. The final outcome, the birth of a son, is secondary to Ruth's love. As the women of Bethlehem sing to Naomi they remind her, "Your daughter-in-law who loves you . . . is better than seven sons!" The Book of Ruth reunites the tribes of Israel by joining the houses of Rachel and Leah under a single blessing, wherein the mothers of Israel are affirmed as the cobuilders of the nation.

Ruth's famous words of loyalty to Naomi are often quoted at weddings and conversions. I would like to restore them to their original context as an oath of love between women to care for each other and to create community as a source of sustenance throughout the years.

7. Final blessings

We sing another song and play our drums. Then we uncover the bread, a braided round challah with a rose in the center and roses around the sides. We say the blessing over the bread and enjoy the feast we have assembled. The women who have participated in this ceremony become eligible to light the Rosh HaShanah candles and initiate the people into the new year.

Honoring the Years

Honoring the Years is a project based on the work of Barbara Mierhoff, may her memory be a blessing, who documented the importance of storytelling and ritual among the Jewish elderly in Venice, California. Honoring the Years requires the creation of a book, a kind of album of memories that can become part of a congregation's library. I find it extremely frustrating that we have so few texts written by women. My hope is that this ceremony will encourage the writing of firsthand accounts to document the lives of women in our midst.

1. Creating a book about women

People interested in this ceremony should meet several times with a local anthropologist and a social worker whose special focus is aging to develop an approach to gathering oral history that is sensitive and supportive. Barbara Mierhoff's book *Remembered Lives* and Susan Starr Sered's book *Women as Ritual Experts: The Religious Lives of Elderly (Kurdish) Jewish Women in Jerusalem* can be read as background material.

After developing a method for taking oral histories, a group of elder women and their "scribes" meet several times to share memories and mementos around specific themes, which can include memories of childhood, coming to America, sayings and stories about female relatives, recipes, incidents around being Jewish, lessons learned about the nature of life. Poetry, letters, photos, and other objects can also be shared (and photographed). Then the scribe and the elder assemble a book from these transcripts and photos.

2. The ceremony

The whole congregation is invited to a Sunday afternoon potluck ceremony. The menu can be determined by the elders. The congregation sings welcome songs. Each elder is presented with her book by the scribe who has been recording her words. The elder will already have chosen one or two incidents from the book to recount on this occasion. After the sharing, each elder is presented with a gift from the congregation. Final songs are sung and the meal is served. The books are displayed during the meal and social time. This prayer can be offered at the end of the ceremony:

A Prayer for the Elder Woman

In the tradition of Sarah and Serach,

Miriam and Devorah,

The wise women of Avel and Tekoah,

And the prophet Hulda,

Your words and memories are a blessing

In the hearts of the people.

May Shekinah be with you all the days of your life.

May you come and go in peace and joy.

Know that the seeds of wisdom you have planted

   on this day

Will continue to bear fruit in the lives of those present.

You are like a mighty tree growing beside still waters.

Your roots are deep, your crown wide,

And we, gathered under your shade, are blessed.

Blessed by the wise women of Israel,

We glorify Her name.

Part Four

COMMUNITY

COMMON EFFORTS
TO PROMOTE NONVIOLENCE

Communities of support are the antidote to despair. One such community grew out of the events around the 1981 U.N. Disarmament Conference, which attracted more than one million people to the streets of New York City. At the time I was working as the staff person for the Jewish Peace Fellowship, which is a member organization of the Fellowship of Reconciliation. The JPF and FOR are committed to nonviolent activism as a method of social change. Both groups are dedicated to overcoming the violence in our lives by working to end war and secure human rights. Members of the Jewish Peace Fellowship believe that Jewish values and historical experiences can provide inspiration for a nonviolent way of life.

My job that year was to work with a group representing scores of religious and ethnic communities throughout the world to create an all-inclusive worship service. The result was a magnificent weaving of songs and prayers about disarmament. Ten thousand people gathered inside St. John the Divine Cathedral to pray together. One truth encircled us in faith and hope: the truth of our common humanity reflected in our love of children and the earth. This truth ignited our desire to work together to end war and violence and to be active in the pursuit of these ends. I was especially inspired by people whose entire lives were committed to securing social justice and an end to violence in society. I especially remember Thich Nhat Hanh, a Buddhist monk from Vietnam, a one-hundred-year-old Hopi elder named Grandfather David, and Naomi Goodman of the Jewish Peace Fellowship. All of them emerged from their struggles with deep compassion and an enduring devotion to peace. Their lives and the lives of others who give their time on earth to the pursuit of caring and just societies are a spiritual beacon in our midst.

The pursuit of justice as a central religious demand in the practice of Judaism was first taught to me by the Reform rabbis of my youth, and especially by Rabbi Stephen Schaefer. I grew up during the civil rights movement of the 1960s and witnessed the social activism of the Reform rabbis who worked with teens. They encouraged our activism by emphasizing the prophetic traditions of Judaism, including the words of Amos, Hosea, Isaiah, and Micah, along with the Passover story and the code of behavior in Leviticus 19, which commands us "to love our neighbor as we love ourselves."

Not until I entered the feminist movement, however, did I appreciate the role of women in the worldwide struggle for peace. Feminism taught me to apply the concern for justice voiced within my tradition to women's lives, and to listen to women's perspectives on issues of injustice that occupy their time and energy.

There are many problems that need our attention. As Jews we are obligated by our religion to pursue justice actively. One religious goal for Jews today is the creation of institutional and personal relationships based on partnership rather than on hierarchies of gender, class, religious affiliation, or ethnic background. Another goal is the perpetuation of a viable and diverse Jewish culture that celebrates our creativity.

In all these efforts I have come to adopt the philosophy of nonviolence, which I have learned through involvement with the Jewish Peace Fellowship, the Fellowship of Reconciliation, and feminist circles such as Greenham Women. I see nonviolent activism and the effectiveness of its campaigns over the years as a natural corollary to the prophetic tradition and belief that "not by might and not by power, but by spirit alone shall we all become free." Women have a special stake in the perpetuation of nonviolence as a peacemaking philosophy because women suffer the brutality of war and the sexual violence it both instigates and excuses, whether on the home front or on the battlefield.

Jewish women must also question the new mythologies of empowerment that have been generated by the state of Israel as one response to the destruction of the European Jews. Empowerment has been translated as militarism and machismo, which has channeled Jewish resources into the funding of an enormous military establishment that does not in any way support the lives of women. As a woman, I feel the need to resist the notion of empowerment as the right to commit violence. I seek positive strategies and religious directions that affirm women's right to safety and security as a central part of Jewish cultural concern. I call on Jewish women and men to become involved at every level in the work of creating a Jewish peace culture that also has as its focus the condition of women's lives.

THE ISSUES IN "COMMUNITY"

In this part I offer a framework for action around the three issues that concern me most. The first is the ruination of so many ecosystems throughout the world, and its impact on women's lives. The Torah can be viewed as a plea to create a system of law that places the condition of those who suffer poverty at the top of our hierarchy of concern. Currently the ongoing plundering of the earth's precious resources forces women to spend most of their days in hard labor simply to gather fuel and water. The first portion of part 4 outlines seven mitzvot, or sacred obligations, meant to help us structure our response to this serious injustice. It also furnishes the reader with practical suggestions for organizing communities in support of women.

My second concern is the tendency of Jews to see ourselves in history primarily as Holocaust victims. This affects our responses to anti-Semitism, to the non-Jewish community, and to the Palestinian people. I will suggest the necessity of a different approach to overcoming the trauma of the Holocaust, an approach that promotes compassion and hope instead of more fear and despair.

Finally I would like to address the question of our relationship to Jewish men in our own time by sharing a series of personal stories that highlight the humorous and hopeful moments of my journey as a woman rabbi and offer exercises to guide us toward working through the painful issues between us with a sense of humor.

I conclude part 4 with a series of rituals dedicated to healing the wounds caused by sexual abuse. Crimes of sexual violence harm our psyche in devastating ways. Jewish tradition forbids the violation of our bodies but does not offer any ceremonies for the victims. These ceremonies constitute a Jewish response to this deadly crime.

13
Eco-Kashrut: Loving the Earth's Body

When HeShe awoke
Yehoyah appeared
And led them to the Living Tree
Whose splendid branches
And green leaves
Sustained the multitudes
Beneath Her gentle canopy.
"See My works?
How fine and beautiful they are?
So think upon this,
Do not destroy My world,
For if you do,
Who will come after
And set it right?"

(Adapted from *Ecca Rabbah*)

The earth is an endangered species. Her forests and plains, mountains and valleys, deserts and wetlands, her fish and fowl, four-leggeds and creepy crawling things, her soil, water and air—all that grows and lives is endangered. Thousands upon thousands of living creatures in every country are burned, gassed, shot, poisoned, tortured, starved, and delivered into extinction day by day. And we, the pinnacle of creation, are committing the murder.

Some of us stand by, enjoying our comfort while we watch the news on TV. Some of us try to respond by engaging in modest alterations of our consumer lifestyle. We might recycle glass or install water-efficient toilets. This is a beginning. Some of us feel overwhelmed by the scope of the problems, and we despair. All of us North Americans who enjoy the privileges of the middle class reap comfort and even profit from the devastation of the earth. For the moment. Yet every time we eat red meat, drive our cars, use styrofoam, buy foods wrapped in plastic, take long showers, and perform a host of other daily actions, we contribute to the degradation of our planet and the erosion of life on earth.

We have been warned before. The Torah tells a story of a flood that devastated our earth long ago. The storytellers say it was brought on by human violence. After the waters receded, Shekinah wove a coat of many colors from the souls of all the creatures who perished in the flood and draped it across the heavens. As the sun glistened on the waters, the human remnant raised their eyes and beheld the rainbow. Shekinah spoke to them once again:

> *"This rainbow is the sign I give,*
> *A covenant between me and you*
> *And every living creature that is with you*
> *For all your generations.*
> *Behold the rainbow!*
> *It is a sign,*
> *A covenant between me and the earth."*

The rainbow reminds us of our kinship with all creation. In New Mexico the rainbows are plentiful. I gaze at a double rainbow shimmering above the Sandia Mountains during an afternoon rain and I am filled with awe at the earth's beauty. I love the desert. I fear in its destruction.

ECO-KASHRUT: DEVELOPING A PRACTICAL GUIDE

This chapter is meant to encourage more people in the Jewish community to fiercely defend the earth. Our growing environmental awareness has added a new dictate: Thou shalt be ecological.

Ecology affirms the interrelatedness of all living beings. The Jewish idea of the Great Mystery as the force that binds all of us in the unity of Being, in oneness, is akin to the ecological concept of the interrelatedness of life. At the same time, ecology teaches us that life is incredibly complex and depends on diversity of being. If we do not honor the complexity and diversity of nature, we are doomed to destroy nature and ourselves. In the search to link Judaism's concerns with the sanctity of life to contemporary concerns about the future of the planet, my teacher Rabbi Zalman Schacther coined the term *eco-kashrut* to describe a Jewish approach to organizing our daily choices so that we can actively engage in ecologically responsible living.

Keeping kosher is a practice familiar to most Jews and non-Jews, although it is neither widely practiced nor understood. Keeping kosher refers to what is permissible for use, *treyfe* refers to that which is not permissible for use. The standards that define permissible use are based on ethical considerations. The primary ethic of Jewish practice is the mandate to act compassionately toward all living beings and not to cause harm or suffering to others. Love of the Great Mystery is demonstrated not by belief or words but in the actions of daily life and the way we treat humans and animals—all sentient beings. Keeping kosher was primarily a way to regulate our behavior along these lines. The practice of separating milk from meat, the laws of kosher slaughtering, the prohibition against killing a mother and her young on the same day, the prohibition against hunting for sport and even against plucking feathers derive from the mandate to live compassionately and avoid causing harm.

In addition, keeping kosher, or determining what is fit to use, is also based on the principle of not deriving pleasure or benefit from goods that have been produced through the pain and oppression of others. One year Levi Yitzhak of Berdichev declared all the matzahs treyfe because of the poor working conditions of the women in the matzah factory. Many people boycott table grapes because they are grown at the expense of farmworkers' health. Reframing kashrut from an ecological perspective widens the scope of kashrut's concerns to embrace our contemporary situation.

I would like to honor my first role models and teachers in the way of what is now called eco-kashrut: Everett and Mary Gendler. From Rabbi Gendler I learned to integrate ecological practices, vegetarianism, nonviolence as a form of Jewish social activism, and my budding feminism. In the late 1970s I visited Everett and Mary on their five-acre farm in Massachusetts. With snow on the ground and bitter winds blowing, we toured the winter rye, the still-hardy kale patch, the extensive hibernating gardens, the compost heap, the root cellar, the circle of stones Mary had arranged for women's gatherings, and the stoic New England woods. Later I browsed through the extensive book and magazine collection in Everett's garage/study, which included publications on the feminine in Judaism, *Akwasasne News* from the Iroquois Nation, Ghandi's writings, mail order catalogs from organic farms, *Keduhat Levi, Etorai Torah,* and the usual mountain of rabbis' literature along with a hearty collection of poetry and secular literature. From Everett I learned to take risks on behalf of those who suffer the ravages of injustice. Everett was the first rabbi I met who openly and honestly addressed the issues of Palestinian rights, gay and lesbian rights, feminist rights, and environmental realities within the mainstream Jewish community. A few years later, during another visit to the farm, Everett showed me the first solar-powered eternal light in Jewish history hanging above the ark in his congregation's shul. Ecology and Jewish spirituality had merged.

The practice of eco-kashrut, or keeping kosher from an ecological perspective, is based on seven sacred obligations, or mitzvot:

1. Honor the Mother: Kavod HaEm

2. Offer hospitality: Kabbalat Panim

3. Save life: Pikuach Nefesh

4. Do not be wasteful: Bal Tashcheet

5. Be kind to living creatures: Tza'ar Baalei Hayim

6. Do not oppress others economically: Lo Tonu

7. Keep the Sabbath: Shmirat Shabbat

HONOR THE MOTHER

Feminism has taught us to see the degradation of the earth and the economic oppression of women as intimately related circumstances. Eco-kashrut begins with love of the body, especially the body of Mother Earth—Cavod HaEm. In Jewish writings the feminine gender and its attributes are identified with the material world, an inferior element in the physical-spiritual dichotomy. We need to transform our relationship to Mother, body, and earth and erase the notion of bodyearth and woman-body as inferior elements in creation. In Hebrew the word for compassion and womb share the same root: *R-Ch-M*. The womb of the earth is our shared place of origin, and so our shared connection to life. Mother-womb is the place of emergence. I offer this poem as a mediation and an explanation for keeping kosher as Kavod HaEm—Honoring the Mother:

✎ *Honoring Kinship, Honoring the Mother*

Rechem, soft and gentle womb
Rachamim, those sharing the same womb
And so, loving compassion for all our kin.
O fiery star who bore us,

Shekinah of vast array,

You demand from us the question

How can we violate the Mother?

Her sons and daughters

Our sisters and brothers—

Are we not all kin?

Thus it is written

Thou shall not seethe a kid

In her mother's milk

Milk from her body

Freely given

But flesh and blood

As food

Forbidden

1. Honoring the Mother by Putting up a Mezzuzah

Honoring the Mother can be ritualized by fastening a mezzuzah on the doorway of your house and on the entranceway to all your rooms. The mezzuzah usually features one of the less well-known names of God inscribed on the cover, that is, Shaddai. Shaddai means "protector" or "guardian." It also means "my breast." Alice Hiat, one of the women artists in my congregation, designed a door of many breasts in honor of women's nurturing function. Seeing the mezzuzah can remind us that the earthbody is our home. How we treat the body of the earth is a primary measure of our spirituality. As we enter and leave our house, even as we go from room to room, let us not lose sight of our home in Mother Earth. Perhaps we should place mezzuzahs on the gateways to wilderness lands, to national forests, to city parks, and to our neighborhoods to remember that the whole earth is our home.

Suggested ritual action: Create a mezzuzah from clay or other material and paint a "feminist mezzuzah" with earth-oriented symbols.

Organizing Events to Honor the Mother

Honor the Mother also implies honoring the Mother's work: to nourish her children, to provide them with food, and to teach them how to use their resources wisely. Keeping kosher is mostly about the way we eat and how we decide what comes to the table. What has been lost for women, however, is our political power as distributors of food and community resources as well as the opportunity to interpret the symbolism of the food we serve.

In biblical times, "mother," or *em,* was a political title. A woman who carried the title "Em Yisraeli" (a mother of Israel) served the nation as a political and religious leader. She could determine the fate of her tribe, her city, and her people through her decision-making powers. In the Second Book of Samuel, the Em Yisraeli of Avel chastises David's general Yoav with these words: "They used to say in ancient times, go seek counsel at Avel, and thus they ended the matter. I am one of those who are peaceable and faithful in Israel. You seek to destroy a city and a Mother of Israel; why will you swallow up an inheritance of YHVH?" (2 Samuel 20:18, 19). The hachama, or wise woman, of Avel reminds Yoav of her position's sanctity among the tribes, of her role as a decision maker for her people, and of the holiness of her role as Mother Israel.

The prophet Devorah is also called Em Yisrael, and she too directs the course of the nation. An Em Yisrael often resided at the summit of a hill or mountain, in the midst of a sacred grove. Her functions included oracular pronouncements. The name Devorah, or Queen Bee, a play on words meaning "Oracle Giver," is probably a title and not a proper name. As Queen Bee and Oracle she sits at the center of her tribe as political and religious leader and conducts the affairs of the people.

Women need to reinvest themselves with the title and political power of Em Yisrael. Our own motherhood has been limited. We secure, prepare, and serve food at the family table. Let us widen the scope of our powers and recognize the true significance of collecting and distributing resources. Let us become guardians of the Mothersource, the earth, the body of the Mother, and demand equal power as we decide future uses of the earth's bounty. An Em Yisrael does not only serve tea and cookies at Friday-night oneg Shabbats but also determines national policy.

We must also honor the men who plant and harvest gardens, who cook and serve food to their families, who care and nurture children, who do the laundry, whose loving heart and hands embrace the compassionate aspect of their human nature, and who are dedicated to a humbler existence through the equitable sharing of resources and the power to decide how resources are used. Here are some practice exercises for observing the mitzvah of Kavod Em:

1. Women's groups within congregations often raise substantial funds for congregational projects. Ask yourselves in what ways you participate in determining how those funds are used and whether they contribute to the educational and material support of women.

2. Another responsibility of sisterhoods is providing food for Sabbaths and special occasions. Ask yourselves in what way this function is shared by the men in your community.

3. Em Yisrael was once a political title. Are there women in your congregation who might carry this title? And what would that mean to the functioning of your community?

4. What do your synagogue grounds look like? Is there a way to set aside land for community gardening, to plant an orchard, to create an indoor greenhouse, or to build a bird sanctuary?

5. Conduct an education series on the ecological impact of local major industries on the lives of women. Investigate how you can serve as advocates for women.

OFFER HOSPITALITY

Enabling people and living creatures to feel secure in their homes and bodies is the concern underlying the second sacred obligation of eco-kashrut: offering hospitality. Making others feel welcome was cited by the sages as the reason Abraham and Sarah were chosen to be the ancestors of a new people. According to the storytellers, Abraham waited by the door of his tent at all hours so he could see people coming from a great distance and run to greet them. Sarah, it was told, kept her tent open on all four sides so that travelers coming from all directions would see her hearth fires burning and feel welcome. Sharing our immediate resources, our love and material wealth, with an open hand and a giving heart is a requirement of Jewish practice.

Hospitality is the ability to give things away because one has replaced the idea of ownership with the concept of stewardship. A steward is a guardian who equitably distributes that which is available, who provides sanctuary and shelter, extends a warm welcome to her guest, and makes strangers feel at home.

Exercises for Creating Hospitable Communities

1. One question for Jewish communities to ponder is, Who do we not make welcome in our midst, and why? As we create new strategies for solving the problems of economic injustice and racism, let us begin by examining our own communities.

    You might schedule a day-long community retreat in which to explore responses to the question of who feels welcome and unwelcome and why. I often work with a skilled mediator when the community meets. A mediator is someone who is committed to impartiality, has a knowledge of negotiation skills, and can help a group resolve the current discussion and define the next step.

2. I have always been drawn to create a community with unaffiliated Jews who, for their own reasons, do not feel welcome in the "organized" Jewish community, whether in religious or secular institutions. I have found the more open a community is to the many voices within it, the freer people feel to be themselves and to share their particular gifts.

    In particular I have been drawn to the work of artists in the creation of community. For me the presence of artists in the community is a priceless gift for us to nurture and draw on. Call all the

artists of your community together in someone's home for the purpose of sharing work and ideas. Look for ways to link local Jewish
artists and visiting artists. Create an artist's celebration of holy
days. Discuss ways that artists can be nurtured by the community.

3. Network with women in prison, in detention homes, in shelters.
   Find ways you can support women in these settings.

4. Use Sukkot, the fall harvest holy day, as a time to focus on the
   obligation of hospitality in our tradition. Each year Jewish people
   build a temporary fall harvest hut called a sukkah in which ceremonial meals are eaten and prayers are said. One custom of the
   holy day is to invite the spirits of biblical ancestors into the sukkah.
   At Nahalat Shalom we have created two large masks representing
   Sarah and Abraham. They enter the sukkah and tell the stories of
   hospitality associated with them in the Bible, folksong, and legend.

5. Create a Friday night Sabbath with the theme of hospitality and tell
   stories of women who have demonstrated tremendous hospitality
   to you.

6. It is customary to greet a guest with the phrase "Brucha Ha-ba-ah"
   (Blessed is she who comes here). The visitor responds, "Brucha
   HaNimtzet" (Blessed is she who dwells in this place).

SAVE LIFE

"I have set before you life and death, blessing and curses; therefore
choose life so you and your children may live" (Deuteronomy 30:19).

A Pueblo woman who visited Colombia on an educational mission
related an incident about a Colombian man who was dedicated to preserving life. This man approached her and four other teachers and asked
if he could borrow their labor and their truck for a certain task. They
immediately agreed. He then gave them each a ten-gallon jug and asked
them to fill each one with water and load them on the truck. They com-
plied and boarded the truck, with him behind the wheel. He drove for

hours through the jungle, having left the marked road. They began wondering about their destination and the sanity of their driver.

Finally he parked the truck on the side of a mountain and began bushwhacking his way down. They followed, lugging their ten-gallon loads for about another hour. Finally they came upon five young trees bravely clinging to the side of the mountain. The man explained that they had been planted by the Colombian government as part of a reforestation project, then abandoned. If they were not watered with some frequency, they would die. After dousing the trees, they returned to the village awed and humbled by this man's straightforward devotion to life. Of this man it may be said, "With all your heart, with all your soul, and with all your might."

Responsible Consuming

Saving life is the supreme measure of our devotion to life. As this story demonstrates, saving life is not limited to human life. Under the category of Pikuach Nefesh we name as treyfe, or unfit for use, those products that endanger life on earth. We name as treyfe products that contribute to deforestation—of rain forests and wilderness—products that lead to species extinction, products that deplete the ozone layer, products that poison the water, the air, and the soil and thus the species who suffer the effects of these poisons, and products that abet the proliferation of war and violence against humans and animals.

How do we begin to list which products fall under Pikuach Nefesh and that must therefore be avoided? Each synagogue, Havurah, or Jewish community institution could form an eco-kashrut council to consider each of these categories and develop a list of eco-kosher and eco-treyfe products. A green magen David with a tree symbol in the center can be the sign of an eco-kosher product that is permissible.

MEDITATION FOR SHOPPING

Stand before the product you are about to buy. Consider the entire process that brought this product to you.

- Where did this product come from?

- What form did this product have in its original state?

- How was it produced?

- Who was involved in its manufacture?

- How were the workers paid?

- Who shipped the product to market?

- Does this product harm or benefit life?

- How will this product be disposed of when you are finished using it?

- Is there another product that is more beneficial to the overall environment that you could use instead of this one?

- Does the company that makes this product engage in other harmful activities, even if this product is benign?

Then as you take the product from its place to pay for it, you say, "In buying this product may I not cause harm. Amen."

Redeeming Captives

Another dimension of saving lives is the obligation to redeem captives. People who are being held in some way as hostages require our activism on their behalf. We need to ask ourselves, Who is being held hostage in our communities, in the world? How can we respond? Inadequate health care, housing, and education are holding many people hostage to poverty and violence. How can we contribute our energy and resources to the transformation of this situation? Are there adequate job training programs for young women in your community? How can you get involved?

Hold vigils for people suffering the ravages of war, massive violence, torture, starvation, and death. We need to raise money for medical supplies, food, and clothing. We need to write letters to the appropriate authorities. We need to be well informed by those who suffer. We need to remember them on all our holy days. Nahalat Shalom and Congregation B'nai Israel of Albuquerque, for instance, sponsored a New Year of the Trees celebration with a Croatian Jewish artist named Toni Franovic, who created breathtaking scenery for a Kurdish Jewish folktale collected by folklorist Howard Schwartz named "The Healing Leaves." We raised money for a medical clinic in Bosnia and sent letters to President Clinton as part of the day's activities.

I would like to offer a model prayer service for a public vigil:

1. A diverse group of people is represented at the vigil through the process of networking and coalition building.

2. A public place is chosen as the site of the vigil, and the news media is contacted.

3. A person from each group represented at the vigil gives an opening prayer to call people together and to reflect the theme of the occasion. For instance, Nahalat Shalom sponsored a vigil and an interfaith Passover seder on behalf of refugees from Central America seeking sanctuary in the United States. Each group represented offered a prayer on the theme of freedom and sanctuary. The participants were from the African American church community and the Arab Anti-Discrimination Committee, they were Hispanic Catholics from various parishes, Baha'is, Korean Christians, and so forth. The event strengthened our ties and raised a thousand dollars in bond money for a refugee who had been imprisoned in the U.S. for illegal entry.

4. A speaker is designated to present information about the current situation of the vigil's particular focus. Eyewitnesses can provide powerful testimony.

5. The community joins in song in the language of the people who are the focus of the vigil.

6. The names of those who have died as the result of violent acts are read aloud. This is followed by prayers for peace from each group represented at the vigil.

7. The vigil concludes with suggestions of action the people can take (signing petitions, writing letters, collecting money, passing out information about what to do) and a song.

DO NOT BE WASTEFUL

The prohibition against wanton destructiveness and wastefulness derives from a mitzvah in Deuteronomy that bars the felling of fruit trees for siege when engaged in battle. The Talmud expanded this notion to apply to someone who leaves his oil lamp covered or naphtha lamp uncovered, thus wasting fuel, or to someone who throws away uneaten food. According to the Talmud, the sacred obligation to pay attention to correct use and not to be wasteful is to be taught to children from an early age in order to reinforce the habit of conservation and repair.

The question of what is essential to living is a question we in North America do not often ask. Yet we use over 40 percent of the world's resources while constituting only 6 percent of the world's population. We are clearly the ultimate wastemakers. Who pays for our overindulgence? Most third world women and children. As we cut down forests to provide room for our factories, women are forced to work harder. Trees provide the majority of the world's people with fuel for cooking, washing, and heating. The massive deforestation brought on by our high comfort needs forces women to walk great distances for wood. Some women rise at 4:00 A.M. and work until 10:00 P.M. just to accomplish basic household tasks. We not only waste trees, water, and soil and pollute the air, we also increase the burden on women's lives manyfold.

Therefore we need to understand the impact of our energy consumption and reevaluate our use of fuel, water, and all the materials we employ for our comfort. We need to buy in bulk, avoid packaged foods, carry our own shopping bags, use leftover food, compost, grow our own food, buy locally grown produce whenever possible, recycle everything we can, use public transportation, carpool, bike, turn off lights when they are not needed, insulate properly, buy secondhand, and get involved politically to transform industrial pollution, which greatly overshadows all private generations of waste. Minority communities especially feel the impact of the toxic wastes generated locally. Most toxic wastes are buried in poor communities here and in third world countries.

Remedies

Many household tasks fall on women's shoulders. In order not to overburden women when converting homes into eco-kashrut households, your eco-kashrut council may want to develop a model based on partnership in the division of labor. For instance, a few Rosh HaShanot ago, I gave an eco-kashrut sermon. As an example of wastefulness I cited the use of disposable diapers, which are one of the major unrecyclable wastes in this country. One woman complained, however, that the burden of doing the extra laundry would fall upon her, as would many of the other eco-kashrut tasks, such as using bath water for gardening. Clearly we need to address this issue and make sure that the responsibility for becoming eco-kosher is carried by all.

A corollary to avoiding wastefulness is the mandate to repair. One midrash taught that only the high priest could enter the holy of holies in the Temple, with the exception of those who were engaged in repair. The work of repair permits one to enter the most sacred places. Learning to repair, instead of buying new, is an important skill. Many women feel inept at repairing things. Jewish learning might include such courses as repairing furniture, sewing, and using construction tools as part of an eco-kashrut program for boys and girls. Tell stories of women who build things with their hands from around the world.

BE KIND TO LIVING CREATURES

Ah, the wisdom of children who have not yet perfected the art of justifying immoral behavior with religious ideology. I became a vegetarian at the age of twenty-seven for the purpose of keeping kosher, eating a more healthful diet, and avoiding beef, which I knew caused massive pollution and poverty in the world. When I gave birth to Nataniel, his father and I decided to feed him a vegetarian diet. Nataniel loves fruits, vegetables, grain, tofu, beans, and rice and will try anything once.

At the age of four he asked me why we didn't eat meat. Nataniel loved our cat, Rosh HaShanah (named for the day on which the cat adopted us), and the first answer that popped into my head was, "Well, would you eat Rosh HaShanah? Every animal has a personality, feelings, and a desire to be free, just like Rosh HaShanah." Nataniel understood immediately and seemed to need no further explanation.

A few months later, we visited my sister in New York City. While cruising around the South Street Seaport, we stopped for lunch. Jan ordered a hot dog and was about to sink her teeth into the bun when Nataniel piped up, "Aunt Jan, who kills your meat for you?" The effect of that question was profound. Who kills for us? If we witnessed the death of the animals we eat, could we continue to eat them?

A story from the Talmud is told of Rabbi Judah the Prince, editor of the Mishnah, amid a discussion about the meaning of suffering, and, in another place, as a commentary upon the verse "And Elohim remembered Noah and all the animals." Once Rabbi Judah was sitting outside the synagogue in Sepphoris, occupied with the study of Torah. A calf on its way to slaughter broke free and hid under Judah's robes. Rabbi Judah pulled the calf out and handed her over to her master. It began crying as if to say, "Save me from this slaughter!" Rabbi Judah said to it, "What can I do? For this you were created." The calf was led away. For this act of heartlessness, Judah was punished from heaven with thirteen years of toothache. The mouth that taught Torah and chewed meat was denied the pleasure of both. What redeemed him? One day his daughter discovered a nest of weasels in the house while sweeping and was going to remove them when Judah quoted her the verse from Psalms, "YHVH has mercy on all of His works!" She desisted and let them stay. For this Rabbi Judah was restored to health.

Jewish tradition regards the shedding of animal blood as a moral shortcoming. The intricacy of the laws of kashrut are meant to inhibit

meat eating. The slaughter of animals was believed to lead to human violence against other humans as well. But, more important, the life of the
animal was valued in and of itself. There are countless Jewish stories and
legal guidelines testifying to Jewish sensibilities about animals. For instance, one can be paid for loading up a beast of burden but not for un-
loading, as this is a religious obligation. One should not harness two
different kinds of animals to the same plow, as one of them might be in-
jured. One is enjoined to feed one's animals before feeding oneself.
Some sages prohibit the plucking of feathers, and most prohibited hunting for sport. Even if one sees the beast of one's enemy tottering under a
burden or lost, one is obligated to relieve the animal and return it.

Furthermore there is no special blessing for the eating of meat, although there are blessings for eating fruits and vegetables. The strictures
around eating meat, and the laws dealing with kindness to animals, have
led many Jews to vegetarianism over the centuries, from the hasidim of
Yehudah the Pious in the 1200s to Isaac BatSheva Singer and Rav Kook
in our own century. Recently many hundreds of Jews have taken up vegetarianism in their pursuit of Jewish spirituality. In our own time, the
cruelties involved in the factory farm production of meat would seem to
prohibit the eating of it. If the goal of kosher slaughtering is to kill the
animal so it feels no pain, then this is an impossible task in our day. Your
eco-kashrut council might want to sponsor a tour of a slaughterhouse.
After such a tour, I can't imagine that anyone would want to continue to
cause such suffering.

In ancient times, Shekinah, as the Goddess, was Lady of the Beasts.
Everywhere in the ancient Near East the Goddess stood on lions or was
surrounded by gazelles or took the shape of a bird. Shekinah's body is
the body of living creatures, the body of our kin. The lions that guard
the entrance to the holy of holies are the lions of Shekinah. She, like
they, is wild of heart and untamed. To be holy is to be wild, to let the
fires of the spirit burn freely, to be true to one's spirit nature. Eco-
kashrut means giving back to the earth its wildness, opening our hearts
to the needs of the wild, and being redeemed into our own humanity by
respecting the ways of the earth. Let us find common cause in the pro-

tection of habitat and enter networks with people worldwide who are balancing the need for economic sustenance with the right of all creatures to their homes.

Suggestion for Action

Judaism celebrates four new years, one of which is the new year for animals on Rosh Hodesh Elul, the moon before Rosh HaShanah. Although this holy day has fallen out of use, it was a time during which animals were set aside for tithing purposes. We might rededicate Rosh Hodesh Elul as a time to honor our relations with the creatures of the earth. In Santa Fe every year there is "creatures day parade" in which each person dresses as her or his favorite animal. Skits are performed and information is shared about the various animals represented. This might be a way of coming together in Elul or during the week in which the story of the flood is read in the synagogue.

DO NOT OPPRESS OTHERS ECONOMICALLY

In Leviticus 19:13 we read: "You shall not oppress your kin nor steal from him [or her]." The word *re-echa* is a kinship term that goes beyond blood ties. It includes in its sphere the entire human community. *Lo tonu* calls us to create societies that apply their resources to remedy the condition of the poor.

The Torah pays special attention to economically vulnerable women. Women are listed in the category of "widow" along with orphans, landless priests, and landless peoples (the homeless) as those at risk. Widows included women with children, and orphans included children with only mothers. The story of Ruth demonstrates just how vulnerable women in biblical society were to the loss of inheritance, land, and protection when their husbands died. The only road back into security was marriage to a kinsman. Women in Israel still suffer under outdated Jewish marriage laws that forbid women to initiate a divorce and allow men to leave their wives without divorcing them. Jewish women throughout the world continue to address this issue.

The economic oppression of women as a class is still very much with us. In America we have coined the term "the feminization of poverty." Much of this poverty is due to women's role as primary providers for their children. Society asks women not to have abortions but is not willing to provide the material and educational sustenance needed to help women raise their families in dignity. Women also hold most of the low-paying jobs in our society. We are constantly faced with wage discrimination.

Eco-kashrut should include a study of the economic conditions of women of every ethnic background and economic class in our immediate surroundings. Lo tonu should include an evaluation of the Jewish community's relationship to the poor in its midst and should consider economic advocacy as part of its charitable programming. Without a comprehensive evaluation of the economic status of women, eco-kashrut cannot fulfill its goal of a just society.

It is incumbent upon Sisterhoods and other fund-raising groups in organized Jewish life to ask themselves how much of the money they raise goes toward supporting women's projects. Jewish women artists, business entrepreneurs, and educators might be considered the beneficiaries of special funding, interest-free loans, or some other kind of group support. Jewish Family Services might be given funding especially to support rape counseling, battered women, and other special needs that Jewish women may have. We need to combine our resources and focus our energies to serve those women who are marginalized by the mainstream community and require financial assistance.

KEEP THE SABBATH

Shabbat is the central holy day in Jewish life. From Friday evening sundown until Saturday evening upon seeing three stars, we rest from our weekly occupations and dedicate our time to the enjoyment of family, friends, and community, to study and prayer, to feasting, lovemaking, singing and storytelling, to long, leisurely walks and naps, and to communion with our earth home. The word *Shabbat* is derived from the Hebrew word meaning "to return to the resting point," to the center of our renewal. Shabbat embodies the flow of cyclical time and energy, time that vacillates from periods of activity to periods of rest.

On the seventh day the creative process is infused with spiritual intention so the process of creation can be sustained. We return to our creative and spiritual center, the place of regeneration inside ourselves and our relationships. This is accomplished by consecrating our time and activity to the transformation of everyday routine by abstaining from it and fashioning a time focused on pleasuring our senses, our body, our intellect. Jewish tradition regards Shabbat as the culmination of the creative process, when creation reaches its moment of stillness and becomes receptive to subtler energies and insights, which then emerge to form the next level of our creative outpourings during the following week.

Shabbat enjoins us to release people, animals, and the earth from their utilitarian tasks in the world of labor and commerce and to allow all beings leisure time. The purpose of this commandment is to enable us to honor one another's intrinsic value apart from the way we serve one another. During Shabbat we do not plant, harvest, or hoe; neither do we manipulate any of the earth's resources to benefit our needs, other than the simple acts of eating or resting under a shade tree. We avoid the world of commercial exchange by not using money, refraining from shopping, and avoiding the telephone. We also avoid the pursuit of passive entertainment, such as movie going, watching TV, playing computer games, or listening to the stereo. We remove ourselves from our usual pursuits in order to give our full attention to our deepest and most enduring values and our most beloved relationships. Shabbat is a day of "let it be."

Shabbat's spiritual focus includes the overcoming of social hierarchies fixed in gender roles and economic relationships by dissolving them for a twenty-four-hour period and entering a covenant of equality. Everyone is engaged in celebration. The usual hierarchies can then give way to new potentials as we change the context of our usual communication. Each person and being is thus freed from the usual obligations and the elements of oppression those obligations might carry.

Shabbat is a time when we dedicate ourselves to the renewal of our connection to the Jewish people and to Jewish traditions and teachings, which we may invest with enriched meaning. Just as Jewish culture carries the tools to nourish and refresh us, so we open our inner resources to the enhancement of our community and its traditions.

Shabbat can become the perfect vessel for the creation of an eco-kashrut world, a world free of gender, class, and race oppression, a world that is hospitable to animals and children, a world that values the pursuits of the imagination, a world that honors creation. What follows is a Friday night service, to be conducted at home or in the community, that affirms the goals of eco-kashrut and establishes our spiritual intentions.

Recipe for Welcoming the Sabbath

Thursday evening to Friday afternoon: Preparations

A clean house, a dinner party atmosphere, a festive table cloth, flowers, decorations, special glasses, plates, food, and clothing welcome Shekinah, the Beloved Guest, as we prepare to receive her with ceremony and festive adornments. The Friday evening meal can be prepared in advance, the challah baked or purchased, and business details attended to before the weekend begins in order to free our time for celebration. Household tasks should be divided among all the members so that the burden does not fall solely on one person. Perhaps members of your household can arrange to leave work early on Friday afternoons on a regular basis so that Shabbat can be prepared for without the rush.

Prayer for Burning the End Piece of the Challah

With this challah, I honor my mothers,
Who enticed wisdom from grain.
I honor the fire,
Which transforms again and again.
I honor the love that flows through my hands,

And I honor the Spirit

That brings forth this bread from the earth. Amen.

The challah end piece is then burned outside, and the ashes are scattered over the garden, upon the earth.

Rituals of Intention: Mikveh, Tzedakah, and Inviting Guests

Mikveh: See chapter 15, pages 220–221 for an explanation of ritual baths.

In New Mexico, people are fond of hot springs, hot tubs, and the company of good friends to enjoy the pleasures of spiritual soaking. There's nothing like it to relax and "chill out," an essential ingredient in being able to celebrate the pleasures of Shabbat properly. Progressive Jews also need a communal shvitz, a place to soak that is not restricted by Orthodox practice.

Nahalat Shalom is preparing to construct a humble New Mexican shul, and communal baths are on our list of priorities. Sometimes I imagine the Sabbath as the womb of Shekinah, the amniotic fluids of creation. As we enter the mikveh, we reenter the world of beginnings, *Beresheet,* and restore compassion and peace to the process of creation. The mikveh is a gift of renewal, a warm water healing, releasing us, relaxing us, restoring us to joy. Use your breath, meditate in the waters, allow time to purify yourself from the week.

Tzedakah is the term that refers to the sacred obligation to give away one tenth of one's resources to the poor. A Jewish household is incomplete without a tzedakah box on the Shabbat table. Every Friday evening before the festivities begin, make a collection. When the box is full, count it up and give it to a local effort that works for the poor. This does not fulfill your total obligation to give. Every time you receive your paycheck, give some of it away. Tzedakah should be a regularly practiced mitzvah. As Em Yisrael, women have the right and duty to collect and distribute resources from their communities.

Inviting guests: Shabbat would not be Shabbat without a host of guests at our community gatherings or household meals. Guests increase our sense of celebration, especially when they bring their own magic to the occasion through a story, a song, good humor, or simply by being present. Shabbat is also an opportunity to invite into your home the elderly of your community or people staying at a shelter.

The Sabbath Table Ceremonial

Hadlakat HaNerot: Lighting the candles. Our mothers have traditionally initiated sacred times by rekindling the sacred fires of creation. In our own time all are invited to share in the kindling of light.

Prayer at the Kindling of Light

> *Blessed be she who kindles the flames of creation.*
> *Blessed be he who sparks the imagination.*
> *Blessed be those who weave threads of light throughout*
> *the generations,*
> *Who turn our longing for peace into illumination.*
> *[Personal prayers are offered by all those gathered with*
> *the phrase: "I pray for . . ."]*

A story is told that focuses the theme of the evening, connects us to the Torah portion of the week, delights the children, and honors the Sabbath.

Melodies are sung to open the heart. Songs such as "Bim Bam, Lecha Dodi," wordless melodies, or whatever your household knows.

Seven blessings for the Sabbath. Seven is a sacred number among Jewish people and represents our division of time, which honors the seventh day, the seven colors of the rainbow, seven notes in the octave, seven manifest spheres of energy in the mystical tree of life.

1. A blessing for the children. It is a custom for parents and adult friends to place their hands on the heads of the children and recite the following:

↜   ### A Priestly Blessing

May the blessing of peace be upon you.
May love abide with you.
May Shekinah illuminate your heart
Now and forever more.
May you be blessed with . . . [adults fill in with
improvised blessings]

2. Blessing for elders. Elders are the wings of the Shekinah. They enable us to fly. The eldest one present makes a blessing on behalf of the community in his or her own words. Sometimes we ask all those over sixty to make a blessing.

3. Blessing for intimate relations, close friends, lifelong partners. We sing or recite Shir HaShirim, the Song of Songs.

4. Blessing for the sacred day. We sing "Lecha Dodi."

5. Blessing for the earth and all that dwell therein. We sing "Shalom Alechem."

6. Blessing for liberation from injustice. We recite the kiddush over the wine.

7. Blessing for the earth. We recite the blessing over the challah.

The meal is served.

After dinner those gathered join in song and tell more stories, the children go to bed, and intimate partners consecrate their love with scented oil, a couch of romance, and joy.

Shabbat shalom!

14
Healing the Trauma of Jewish History

TO BECOME SUCCESSFUL in our coalition with other peoples, Jews must grapple with the meaning of the Holocaust in our 'ives. How we respond to the Holocaust shapes our ability to relate to other people's suffering. It ultimately influences the direction of our time and energy toward our culture as Jews.

THE SPECTER OF THE HOLOCAUST

Although I read about and saw films about the Holocaust as a child in Allentown, my seven-month stay in Israel in 1966 brought me closer to the reality of the event in people's lives. The Holocaust is often the topic of conversation in Israel. It was a specter hiding in the edges of words, crouching in the silence between sentences, poised to ravish an unsuspecting noun.

The noun *scramble,* for instance, uttered at four o'clock tea as my friend's mother poured. We were chattering about our day at school, the premilitary training course, and our laughable scramble over a wall. Her mother's facial muscles shifted inadvertently. A shadow hovered over her mouth. Suddenly she was a child in Poland reliving the chaos of the war. She huddled in her nakedness with her entire village beside an open grave. Shots exploded, people screamed and collapsed into the pit. She screamed as she fell. Bodies slammed against her, drowned her in flesh and blood. She gasped for air and fainted. Sometime later she snapped awake beneath a pile of corpses. She struggled up a ladder of tangled limbs and shattered faces and groped her way toward the light. What met her eyes as she broke through, I cannot imagine. She did not describe that horror with words, but we saw it on her face.

Somehow she scrambled across the pit of vanquished humans and escaped into the forest. She wandered for days, sobbing, desolate, until miraculously she was rescued by the partisans. My friend had heard this story before and continued to sip her tea, her eyes glued to the floor. I was stunned, and I cried. The Holocaust memory recedes to the shadows of her mother's mind, and she grows quiet.

I tried to absorb the horror, but the catalog of Holocaust brutality is too vast. I went with my Israeli school class to Yad VaShem. We descended the stairs to the exhibit. I had never seen so many photographs, pictures now too familiar. People starved into corpses alongside smiling Nazis, who brandish their sadism unabashed. The beaten ones are my relatives, Jews, slaughtered six million times over. As I gazed into their faces I could not comprehend how people could be so cruel. I was only seventeen and still a child. I was especially drawn to the faces of the Jewish children in the pictures, who still haunt my soul with their hunger, their innocence, their look of betrayal. I heard their question, the question I asked myself: How can adults be so cruel to children? Suddenly I was weeping again, feeling a great sorrow gnawing at my heart. I yearned to make the world over again for these children, to heal their wounds, restore their trust, end their suffering.

The brutalization of children is hardly ever addressed by theologians, politicians, or partisans of ethnic causes. Yet time and time again, children become the principal victims of adult violence in the name of national security, religious doctrine, ethnic solidarity, or economic progress. Let us base Jewish peace culture on kindness to children, because children suffer the consequences of our fears, our hatreds, our greed, and our ignorance. Not only Jewish children deserve our attention. Let us place the children of all peoples on our knees and call them our sons and daughters.

My own encounters with survivors opened my eyes to the pain of others as well. I noticed the fear and betrayal in Joseph's eyes. Joseph was a Palestinian. He sat grasping the edges of his chair in a corner of a community center in midtown Haifa. His face was stormy with emotion; his eyes darted from side to side to make sure no one was eavesdropping. Joseph told me what he had heard from his father and mother: How his family lost their land, their village, their home in 1948; how most of his relatives had been forced to walk to Jordan by Israeli soldiers, and how his grandmother died along the way; how they weren't allowed to return to their village, but his father escaped and remained in Israel. He spoke of the day of reckoning when he and all the Arabs would rise up and take back the land stolen from them. I shivered as I listened to Joseph's words. That year, 1966, I learned the other side of the story of "a people without a land and a land without a people." Most Jewish adults cast Arabs in a very bad light. I inherited that fear, yet I was curious. When I was assigned to write a paper about some facet of Israeli life, I chose Arab Israelis; and Atalah Monsour, the first Palestinian journalist to write for an Israeli newspaper (*Ha-Aretz*), became the one to open my eyes about his people.

I arrived at Atalah Monsour's doorstep in the summer of 1966 with my Israeli host, Shula. I lived with Shula and her Romanian family in their humble three-room house in upper Nazareth. When I told Shula about my intended project, she told me she knew Atalah Monsour. Due to my then-primitive Hebrew and my enthusiastic teenage naïveté, I assumed she meant she knew Atalah Monsour personally. We traveled down the hill to the ancient city of Nazareth, inquired, received directions to Atalah Monsour's house, and were admitted by his wife. Although Mr. Monsour was not home, his wife graciously served us cold drinks and cake in the impeccable style of Palestinian hospitality. When he finally returned, Mr. Monsour was rather miffed at our audacity. Embarrassed, I explained my misunderstanding, apologized for intruding without an appointment, and expressed my desire to learn about Arab Israelis and their life in Israel. Mr. Monsour softened and decided to invest some time in the education of a young American Jewish woman. For half an hour he told me a story I had not yet heard, the account of 1948 and life in Israel from a Palestinian perspective. It was and still is difficult to hear that testimony.

The truth is that we did not proceed as innocents in the beginning of our state building. We ignored the local population, which was the majority. We destroyed over four hundred Palestinian villages and created a refugee population of 780,000 people. We also imprisoned those Palestinians who remained within the Green Line by treating them as second-class citizens, allotting them fewer government goods, taking their land, restricting their travel and military service, and stereotyping them negatively. We created an ideological strategy to achieve the goal of Jewish domination in Israel in which the Holocaust came to justify all our actions, including the development of militarism as a way of life, the domination of Orthodoxy as the state religion of Israel, and the suppression of Palestinian nationalism.

My encounters with the survivors of the European destruction and my absorption of Jewish values such as the pursuit of justice had led me to believe that Jews could not act unjustly toward others. That was, of course, a naive and unrealistic assumption. We are a people like any other people. Mr. Monsour, Joseph, and many other Palestinians throughout the years have taught me that just as Jewish people demand accountability from those who participated in the crimes of the Holocaust whether directly or through inaction, so Palestinians demand accountability from Jews for their actions. Even though the Holocaust cannot be compared to Palestinian experiences in terms of the immensity of the terror, still the events of 1948, the occupation, and the Intifada all demand Jewish self-inspection.

Self-inspection reveals a litany of Jewish misdeeds that grows daily. Stealing water and land, vigilantism, the closing of schools, the appropriation of cultural centers for military use, the denial of medical aid, collective punishment, mass imprisonment, curfews, roundups, shootings, beatings, torture, economic oppression, the destruction of homes, deportations, trial without jury, censorship, and constant harassment are daily features of the Israeli occupation of the West Bank and Gaza and, to a degree, constitute the life of Palestinians living within the official borders of the Israeli state. Those who suffer this brutality the most are children. Thousands upon thousands of children. This is intolerable.

We are a people of nightmares spawning another people of nightmares. Jewish soldiers breaking into Palestinian homes at four in the morning, dragging off parents, brothers, and sisters. Children witnessing their families being beaten, shot, humiliated, occupied. How can we reconcile our two peoples when we are creating generations of Palestinian children who fear us?

Violence is not the antidote to our fears and powerlessness. We cannot claim that the silence of God during the Holocaust means that the prophetic voice of our people is dead or inoperative. Either we are committed to the ethics of justice and peace or we are not. We cannot be authentically Jewish or authentically human if we are comfortable justifying our violence in pursuit of our own empowerment. We must choose.

The truth of Jewish brutality toward Palestinians is difficult to face because we have been so deeply wounded. We carry potent emotions of mistrust and insecurity. Our woundedness may explain our denial, depression, insecurity, and rage, our willingness to see the entire world as a potential oppressor and our inclination to place ourselves in difficult situations. Jews-as-Holocaust-victims is often the only face we show to the public. We do not present ourselves as a creative and dynamic culture of four thousand years that has survived and flourished throughout time, even as we have suffered. It is not our suffering that should distinguish us but the fruits of our religious life. Those who suffer need our courage, and we need our courage as well to overcome the temptation to dwell on our exile as a major theme. Our woundedness must not only be faced with courage; it must be healed through the zealous pursuit of justice based on our tradition of loving the other as oneself, of championing the marginalized and dispossessed, of healing and empowering our children. The challenge facing Jews, as well as all peoples of the earth who have suffered violence, is that of creating a gentler planet in the context of a global vision.

As Jews we have a difficult task ahead of us: to reckon with both our history and our present, to face the Holocaust and its implications for our psyche, and to stand courageously for justice and peace throughout the world. We possess, for the moment, the protection of the mightiest nation on earth. We are not as vulnerable as we once were. The world has come to acknowledge a standard of human rights that includes rights for Jews. We are also sheltered by Christians who have held themselves accountable for their history of intolerance, which led to the persecution of the Jews and fed the flames of the Holocaust. We have in our power at this moment the possibility of offering the world a dream of peace come true.

Women have a special interest in transforming a victim mentality that chooses machismo as the method of defense into a model based on partnership in creation. Women and children face rape, domestic violence, and the loss of their reproductive and political rights in societies throughout the world. Women will not literally dismantle guns, but we can work to dismantle militarism, brutal state policies, and the degradation of human life. Jewish and Palestinian women living in the Middle East have shown the world that it is possible to talk, to work out differences, to build a framework for peace. Jewish women need to keep a spotlight on those efforts. Jewish and Palestinian women cannot afford to see one another as enemies. The survival of our children and our freedom depend on our mutual cooperation.

REMEDIES

During the time of the Holocaust memorial services in town, Nahalat Shalom sponsors an evening service in which people share short readings by those who went through the Holocaust. We light memorial candles and talk about the ways in which the Holocaust has affected our lives. Toward the end of the service we offer spontaneous prayers for peace, with the opening phrase, "I pray for peace in the life of . . ." Finally we read the names of relatives of those in the community who perished in the destruction of the European Jews, and then we recite the kaddish.

One way to emphasize Jewish creativity and strength rather than victimhood is to plan a public program that brings people together around Jewish art. One year Nahalat Shalom sponsored a Jewish arts festival that featured more than fifty artists, including painters, sculptors, weavers, poets, musicians, woodworkers, and fabric artists, whose work explores Jewish themes in some way. Over six hundred people attended! We invited our friends to witness the creative fruits of our tradition. Another facet of that work is our ongoing involvement in local social justice issues. These connections generate relationships not rooted in Jewish self-pity or mistrust of non-Jews. We present a living tradition to the community as well as the memory of our greatest tragedy.

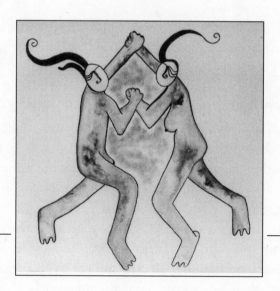

15
Women and Men

IT IS THE LATE 1970s and I am in a conservative shul
in Riverdale, New York. It is decorated with plush paisley
carpeting and crystal chandeliers. The event is a Sunday
morning men's club breakfast, and I am the guest speaker, talking about
"Women and Judaism." The men have graciously invited their wives,
and the place is packed. I presume this is because people are curious to
see and hear a woman rabbi. I'm something new under the sun.

I forgo the dais and the mike and meet the men's club without ob-
structions. Using gentle humor, Talmudic quotes, and stories, I address
the need for change. Afterward an elderly sister of a famous rabbi and
scholar comes up to me, grabs my hand, pulls me down to her level, and
whispers her secret in my ear: "You know, I wanted to be a rabbi like my
brother, but they wouldn't let girls. I'm sorry I was born then and not
now. Be strong." She squeezes my hand tightly. "Do it for all of us who
could not."

To be male in Judaism is to be remembered. To be female is to be penetrated, to leave behind a famous son if possible, and then to disappear from the story.

It is the late 1970s, and I am in a conservative shul in Bayside, Queens. I'm sitting on the *bimah* (pulpit) Saturday morning around Purim time, ready to deliver a sermon titled "Women and Judaism—the Hidden Tradition." Friday evening I had led services in sign language to a warm and receptive crowd in the social hall. As I sit and scan the Saturday congregation, two men walk into the sanctuary, take one look at me, gasp out loud, run back into the hallway, and start screaming. I can even hear their arms flail. A few seconds later, they march up the steps of the bimah, grab my arms, and try to drag me off.

Where is the rabbi? I wonder. No help in sight. With a steely gaze I tell them to remove their hands from my arms immediately. "I mean immediately!" They comply.

"Who let you up here?" they demand. They are both rather short in stature.

I inform them I have been invited by the rabbi to sit on the bimah, and I'm not getting off. "Who am I speaking to?" I ask them. They introduce themselves as the former president of the congregation and the current head of the ritual committee. Finally the rabbi returns and an argument breaks out. As sparks fly, the rabbi cites the custom of stopping services to discuss unresolved grievances just before the Torah reading and suggests we use that custom to discuss this issue. People are becoming embarrassed by the outburst, and everyone grumpily agrees. We daven Shacharit, and I notice the scowls and whispers of the disgruntled watching me daven on the bimah. When the Torah is finally at rest on the reading table, I am invited to give my sermon as a prelude to the discussion. After my prepared talk, I discuss the concept of kavod hatzibur, the practice of honoring the congregation of men by not allowing women a place on the bimah.

It used to be, I explain (citing the volume of the Babylonian Talmud called *Megillah*), that women were called to the bimah for aliyot (to recite blessings before the reading of the Torah). However, it appears that some men felt ashamed in the presence of learned women, so the sages banned women from the pulpit. In our own day, I argue, men have grown to honor and admire women's wisdom as well as their own and no longer feel offended or shamed by women's scholarship. Therefore in our own time this aspect of kavod hatzibur need no longer apply.

I sit down, and the communal discussion erupts with the agitated president of the ritual committee delivering his opinion that women should not be on the bimah because it breaks tradition. He is followed by several other men who agree in a very heated fashion. The comments turn rather nasty. The women in the congregation begin fidgeting. They have never really heard their husbands and male "friends" declare in public with so much apparent lack of reason why women can't ascend the bimah.

Finally an elder woman stands. "I have something to say," she asserts. She points her finger at the Torah curtain. "See that Torah curtain?" she yells. "I embroidered that Torah curtain with my own hands. If she goes [meaning me], then the Torah curtain goes! I've heard enough! It's Shabbos!"

People begin murmuring, It's Shabbos, let's get on with services. I stay on the bimah. The elder woman winks at me. Later that day when I attend the evening service, nine men, including the two who had tried to forcibly remove me, refuse to count me in the minyan and wait ten minutes for the tenth man. The rabbi, bless his soul, was fired several months later for not consulting the proper authorities.

Fifteen years later, I meet a young woman at Bryn Mawr College who looks familiar. She tells me she is the daughter of the rabbi from Bayside now grown up, reading from the Torah, and dating a traditional Jewish man. I realize she resembles her mother, and that is why I feel as if I've met her before. She remembers the incident. I measure my years.

We women are still seeking our place on the bimah. I call women up to the bimah whenever I have the opportunity and invite them to hold the Torah, to read from the Torah, to dance, laugh, and cry with the Torah to overcome their intimidation, sense of shame, fear, and hesitancy about possessing this inheritance as their own. When women hold the Torah for the first time, tears flow in abundance. What was forbidden is now permitted. By whose authority? By our own authority as Jewish women. We say: Let it be so, and it is so. And that is enough.

Each time a woman takes courage and reads from the Torah, Shekinah rises up from the dust, brushes off her ashes, weaves a rainbow tefillin like a wreath of flowers through her hair, displays her glorious wings of fire, and ululates for a minyan of women. She teaches us the old saying: "There is strength in numbers, and the majority rules." We cannot accomplish our task of inclusion and transformation in isolation. We need to stand together. In our local communities, at our national gatherings, in our international efforts, we need to stand together to bind our individual strands and create an unbreakable chain of tradition.

But it doesn't come easily, even when everyone present is a declared feminist. Crossing boundaries into uncharted lands requires improvisation. Some grow afraid. They think crossing over the line means falling into an endless abyss. Everything is challenged, everything is possible. How will we know what works, what doesn't, what saves us, and what damns our souls?

The first meeting of Banot Esh (Sisters of Fire), a group of Jewish feminists, is held in the late 1970s in upstate New York to explore feminism and Judaism. We initiate the retreat by praying a traditional evening service. After the prayers, I raise an uncomfortable question. Why are we davening exactly like the men? How can we explore feminism if we stay within the boundaries of traditional liturgy? I suggest we try something different for Saturday morning Shacharit. Emotions erupt and people cry. Demands are asserted: "I don't feel complete without musaf." "We have to read from the Torah." On the surface there is a conflict between the Reform Jews and the more traditional women. Underneath bubbles unresolved eros between some of the women. Finally we come up with a formula: Each women will bring to Shacharit the essential piece she needs to feel satisfied at the service. Mary Gendler and I search for an outside place (our essential piece) and find a thick rooted tree hovering over a shyly flowing stream with mossy rocks and slippery stones. Some people are hesitant to take the Torah into the forest, but in the end fears turn to smiles, and we see that we can grow and learn from our diversity. As the years pass for Banot Esh, this tenuous beginning is replaced by freer explorations.

✣ What Women Need to Do

Overcome our fear of the wild woman inside us,
invite Lilith to the table,
assert our needs,
let her howl and crackle by the fire,
tell dirty jokes,
walk barefoot in the mud,
open to our rage,
pull out the stops,
delve into the grief of the forest,
remember the power of trees, stones, water, stars, moon,
wolves, snakes, mountains, and the wind.
Once we drink from the well of beginnings,
let us transform our rage and sorrow into creative fires;
let us cook, sew, garden, paint, weave,
dance, drum, write poetry, give lectures,
travel, work with clay,
soak in a hot tub or a mountain stream,
dress to play,
fan the fires that burn within,
be wild,
be practical,
take courses in self-defense and belly dancing,
feel our muscles,

read the Torah from the bimah,

study Hebrew,

engage in discussion, throw our opinions into the fray,

write and lead services,

seek women teachers,

midwife a dream,

have a Bat Mitzvah!

I have just listened to a horrid lecture on the kabbala by an American Jewish man who moved to Israel, converted to hasidism, married a midwife who supports him, has borne him seven children, and stands by his claim that the West Bank belongs to the Jews alone because God gave it to Abraham. His lecture stresses the difference between male and female spirituality in Judaism. The man is the flame that ascends toward life and God. Woman is the opposite. Her energy descends toward earth and death. I raise my hand and ask him if he will quote his sources. He dismisses my question and chastises me for not trusting his pronouncements. He is not interested in discussion, only in his position. "The kabbala's eroticism is only a symbolic representation of diving energies," he assures me, but I am not assured. I wonder what it would be like if women had composed erotic kabbalistic texts, and I decide to give it a try. I compose this kabbalistic fantasy for Rosh Hodesh Shevat, New Moon of the Trees:

❧ *Woman's Kabbala*

loving women loving men

I love women

love to ponder

our feline creases

round and irregular curves

like the earth untamed

ravishing and wild
I relish naked women
in the hot tub
at Rosh Hodesh
we howl
vibrate our bellies
steep ourselves like cinnamon tea
in hot, wet water
women at our ease
relaxing with cherries and wine
waxing philosophical
about trees
sex
and unruly relatives
year after year
stalking our dreams
in the dark of the moon
I tell the women at Rosh
about a poem in which
I imagine a lover
a tall sturdy Scotsman
shadowing his broguish root
and his memories
of male grief with alcohol
raped at seven by a neighborhood man
beaten up by his father for no reason
all this to overcome
he writes a poem

about his mouth

open

to the red flow

of a woman

bleeding on his tongue

he licks her desire

like a piece of flint

pushes his head up her womb

loses himself in her dark interior

where life happens

his soul

humming down her cosmic canyon

he transcends

becomes the alef

expansive and eternal

and she

sobbing with pleasure

brings him back

to the intimate mystery

of her soft lips

I think

if he were hasidic

he would feel guilty

about tasting blood

or avoid his wife altogether

even as she reaches across the table to hand him

a glass of water

he stares at his feet

rather than touch her tainted hand
but my lover is not hasidic
and doesn't care if I'm on top
or if I have my period
delighting like thunder in a storm
he groans
cascading his fruity stream into my desire
where his passion collides and peaks with mine
and today
we don't worry about getting pregnant

In my living room on La Plata Street in Albuquerque, during the summer of 1992, Samantha sits before me. Her Torah portion, Devarim, recounts God's disturbing command to kill all the men, women, and children under Sihon's rule. Sihon would not grant the wandering Israelites passage, food, or water, even at a price. Samantha is horrified by the brutality of the text. She has a hundred questions, which she weaves into her drash. She ponders "why Jews have always been put on a pedestal and why we have ignored the bad stuff about us." She considers the possibility that "Jews just tacked God into the war to justify our battle." She asks, "Why are we hooked on the Torah if there is no definite proof that these things took place? I learned from my mother that we should treat people kindly because we were slaves in Egypt. So why did the Israelites kill the children?"

After much reflection and study of postbiblical commentaries, Samantha comes to several conclusions and observations: Torah is a human text of great literary and spiritual dimensions that challenges us to ask questions, clarify our values, and confront the paradoxes of life. Jewish tradition is constantly reinterpreted by ongoing generations of Jews. Certain values are given more weight over time, and these values are reflected in a family's teachings and lifestyle. Jewish tradition honors questions more than answers.

Samantha takes for granted that her own creativity, perceptions, questions, and additions are a natural part of the weave of four thousand years of Jewish culture, and her involvement and learning will help the tradition endure. She is not yet thirteen. Samantha, like all my Bat Mitzvah students, is living proof of the depth and wonder that awaits Jewish tradition as women contribute their energies to its endeavors. For her Bat Mitzvah Samantha davens Shacharit, plays the drum, signs several prayers, sings a song she has composed, reads a poem she has written, performs a liturgical dance about the Shema, reads from the Torah, and gives a sermon of considerable length.

If Samantha had lived just one generation ago, all this would have been nonexistent. She is the first woman in her family to celebrate her Bat Mitzvah, and sixty out-of-town relatives are traveling to the far reaches of New Mexico for the occasion. Her papa, a puppeteer and teacher, brings her to my house most of the time. Marc is full of humor and sweetness and always offers to buy me fresh fruit from "The Farm" and then never takes the money I offer him. Marc related a story about his grandmother. When she became too old to climb the stairs to the women's section, her grandfather made a place in the back of the men's section. They erected a mini mehitzah—a seven-foot curtain—that she pulled around her. "God forbid the men should see a seventy-year-old woman during prayer," comments Marc. He gives me a photo of Samantha, her mother, Ellen, her grandmother, and her great-aunt posing on the bimah of the Orthodox shul in Hamilton, Ontario. Marc took the picture from the women's section! The women are beaming.

We need the blessings of our fathers as well as our mothers to persevere in our efforts to transform the world into a place that welcomes women. Every time a man makes a pathway for a woman, the Shekinah delights, the angels sing songs, and the ancient throne sends forth a river of light.

I shop for Judaica at an Essex Street store on the lower East Side of New York. Zelig Blumenthal's Judaica shop is so narrow that if I stretch out my arms, I can practically touch both walls. A tiny silver bell tinkles "shalom" as I push open the door. Inside I smell the old country. On one side glass cases rise to the ceiling laden with Torah scrolls, tefillin, prayer shawls, mezzuzot, megillot, sidurim, curled Yemenite shofrot, and Torah pointers. On the other side scores of brass menorahs, candle sticks, havdalah sets, kiddush cups, tzedakah boxes, and cups for the ritual washing of hands are spread across the shelves. In front, another glass case displays Jewish jewelry: dozens of Jewish stars, chais, Hebrew names, mezzuzot on a chain, and tallit fasteners. Zelig is perched on a stool over an open Torah scroll, carefully guiding his feathered quill over a faded letter, an ancient sound.

"Shalom Alechem," I say.

"Alechem Shalom," he answers.

I ask his permission to try out some of the shofrot piled in a cardboard box at the end of the shop. It's almost Rosh HaShanah, and I am high holy day shopping. "Sure," he says. I rummage through the haphazard stack and select a few promising horns, press my lips to the opening and blow. Tekiah, Shevarim, Teruah! I sense Zelig's eyes. I find three shofrot that please me and turn around. Zelig is standing before me, his arms akimbo, a coyote grin on his face. His eyes float large as moons behind thick-rimmed glasses.

"So, you a woman rabbi?" His voice lilts upward and I catch a twinkle in his eye; he's going to test me.

"A student rabbi," I answer, waiting to see what is next.

"Do you have a congregation?"

I tell him about Temple Beth Or of the Deaf.

"Nu, what's your drash for Rosh HaShanah?" He folds his arms and leans against the glass case, interested to learn what this new creature, a woman rabbi, has to say about traditional matters.

I give it a go. I tell him I'm going to talk about the sound of the shofar, its relation to silence, to the sound of creation, the alef, the still small voice, the thunder at Sinai, the words of the prophets, the coming of the end of days. I talk about the deaf community, how they have taught me the power of listening, the mystery of "seeing" voices, which is described as part of the revelation at Sinai, the specialness of blowing the shofar in their presence. I quote some of the sources I'm using: Kedushat Levi, B'nai Yisaschar, and Rebbe Nachman of Bratislav's Sichot HaRan.

Before I utter another word, he claps his hands, whistles the name "B'nai Yisaschar!" and smiles, revealing the large gap between his two front teeth. "Very gut. So, how can I help you?"

I breathe a sign of relief. I've passed his test. He sells me three shofrot for fifty dollars and I know I've made a friend. I visit Zelig often to schmooze and to buy religious articles. He introduces me to his wife and his scribe, and every time I'm in the store, he tells any customer who happens to be there that I'm a woman rabbi working with a deaf congregation.

One time a very Orthodox man in a strimmel (fur hat), white stockings, and black coat enters the shop. Zelig whispers in his ear, pointing in my direction, and the hasid steals a downward glance and nods at me. Zelig grins out loud. He loves to get a reaction.

When my congregation comes to visit the lower East Side on a field trip, Zelig scribes each person's Hebrew name with his quill and ink as a gift.

Once when I want to buy a black-and-white tallit, Zelig takes his own slightly ink-spattered woolen prayer shawl, the one he wears to scribe Torahs, and hands it to me. "Take this," he says. After refusing, acquiescing, and then thanking him profusely, I leave the shop and head in the direction of Gus's Pickles, tears trickling down my cheeks. In giving me his tallit, Zelig somehow gives me permission to continue my work and my struggle with the blessings of my fathers. I smile at the universe for this precious token of love. Soon I learn from a great-uncle that my great-great-grandfather, whose name was Schaefer, was a Torah scribe in Lithuania. The circle comes round.

THE RIGHT TO BE A RABBI

Some people adapt to women's changing roles more easily than others. It is one thing for Orthodox Jews to practice the segregation of women. It is quite another situation for women to face supposedly liberal men in positions of power who claim to be feminists, give lip service to feminist ideas from their pulpits and platforms from time to time, but undermine women's authority when it appears to challenge their own.

When I first moved to Albuquerque, I faced considerable disapproval from some male colleagues, who at first would not speak to me. This abated somewhat due to the help of a woman cantor and another woman rabbi who moved to town several years after I arrived. Unfortunately both women left town the same month for other jobs, and I was once again the lone woman. Soon after their departure, a visiting rabbi and friend revealed one local rabbi's clandestine plot to destroy my career. He was keeping a file on me. I was advised by legal counsel to meet with him and see if I could convince him to desist. I traveled to his turf and met with him in a public place. I realized he meant business and would not change his mind about leaving me alone. He said that if I ever used the title rabbi again, he would expose my charade. The issue for him was my private ordination. I reminded him just how many rabbis were involved in my training, helped me along the way, both in seminary and in the privacy of their homes and studies. I recounted a long list of privately ordained Reform rabbis, as well as the tradition of private ordination among the Orthodox, and mentioned two rabbis who were ordained as I was and were now part of the Reconstructionist Rabbinic Organization and held prestigious positions at major universities. To no avail.

Two days later my name appeared in the local newspaper to announce a workshop I was conducting, and the following day I received a three-page letter that was to appear in the Jewish newspaper. I was given three days to respond to charges that none of my former teachers supported me, that I was a charlatan, that I actually confessed to my persecutor that I was not really a rabbi, that no woman rabbis supported me, and that there was no such thing as private ordination.

I called the board of my community together to assess the situation. First we gained the support of the local Jewish federation, which promised by letter to affirm my ordination and stay out of the fight. Next I called sixty-five rabbis in two days from all around the country, who agreed to sign a letter in support of my ordination, my work, and my contribution to American Judaism. These rabbis represented the spectrum of Orthodox, Reform, Conservative, and Reconstructionist movements; some held institutional positions, some were pulpit rabbis, some were in Hillel, some were seminary professors. I delivered to an intermediary my board's letter, the federation's letter, the letter from sixty-five rabbis (which cost me $365 in phone calls), and my own response. I was told that when he saw the material, he said, "I didn't realize it involved more than just her."

The process of gathering support was very affirming. I spoke to many women colleagues throughout the country who shared similar experiences with male colleagues who were privately and sometimes publicly abusive.

It has taken years of outreach and community building to create a welcome place for myself and Nahalat Shalom among the Jewish institutions and rabbis of Albuquerque. Persistence and belief in ourselves, along with the support of new colleagues in the state, have transformed what began as a hostile situation into a positive climate of intercommunity support for all of us.

I talked about my trials and tribulations with friend and storyteller Marc Levitt in an attempt to figure out the subtext of this strange attack to discredit my work by a man who had never even met me. Marc surmised that the issue was my source of authority. Men in positions of power in the rabbinate, as well as in secular realms, maintain their control by their associations with powerful institutions. They are often at the helm of institutions that grant them access to people with money, large edifices, and secretarial support. I personally have not been able to rely on any of these avenues, since I work at a grassroots level with unaffiliated people who feel so alienated from Judaism that it takes years for them to make even a voluntary high holy day contribution. My "authority" comes from my personal connections with people through my work in storytelling, ritual, and issues of social justice, as well as from the way I translate Jewish values into a contemporary context that embraces feminism.

Although I feel that progress has been made in Albuquerque, the effort to advance women's full creative abilities in the context of Jewish communal life is still often a struggle.

What follows are my words for men who might wish to consider the issue of women's power in relationship to their own.

✍ *What Men Need To Do*

Face your rage
and fear
of that bony woman
who brings the death of an era,
grows flesh on the skeleton of her desire,
and keeps popping up fearsome
until she is properly loved.
Listen for the voice that leads you
to the wild headwaters of your soul.
Dive into the muddy stream willingly
and swim toward the murky dark source,
touch your ecstasy,
let go.
Seek not only the mystical union of energies
described in arcane medieval texts,
but the fresh passion of your sisters' hearts and minds.
Bring us into the domain of male power,
break up the old boys' network
wherever it is,
admit those so long cast out of your interior chambers
without co-opting our language for your own purposes.
Give credit,

enjoy a good time,

cry real tears,

delegate responsibility to your daughters and adult
   women.

Don't depend on old sources of authority to prove your
   point.

Shekinah existed before the law was brought down from
   Sinai.

FREE ASSOCIATION CIRCLE FOR
JEWISH WOMEN AND MEN

This exercise takes about fifteen minutes. It should be followed by a guided evaluation.

   1. Women sit in the middle of a circle surrounded by the men and, through free association, say whatever comes to mind when they think of the phrase "Jewish women." When three or four minutes have passed, they do the same with the phrase "Jewish men." Afterward the men get in the center of the circle and the women sit around them. The men first associate freely with the phrase "Jewish men" and then with the phrase "Jewish women." After the exercise, a mediator already chosen by the group leads the group in the evaluation process.

   2. Retelling the Creation Tale: Read or have someone tell the story of Lilith, the woman created before Eve. Engage in some storyteller's warm-up exercises. Use breathing, explore movement, emotions, characterization. Divide people into groups of five to seven and ask, If Lilith met Eve, how would you tell the story? Give people fifteen to twenty minutes to work out their skit. Then each group presents the results to the others. Afterward evaluate what was presented.

RECOVERING FROM
THE VIOLENCE IN OUR LIVES

During the confirmation hearings of Clarence Thomas, as he sought to become a justice on the Supreme Court in 1992, the American public was forced to face the reality of sexual harassment, a reality many people must endure on a daily basis. Many of us were grieved and enraged as we listened to the comments of the senators and witnesses who challenged the veracity and motives of Anita Hill. Clarence Thomas, by contrast, was allowed his rage and denial. She was required to remain cool and composed.

Whether the victims are male or female, most perpetrators of abuse are male. Many men acquire their sense of power through the domination of children or women. And many men express their need for domination in the most violent of ways: battery and rape.

Sexism is the climate that encourages the abuse of girls and boys, for sexism is the institutional devaluing of women's and children's lives. Even as we teach our children to feel good about themselves, our daughters are developing the internalized notion that they may be less important than boys. Girls learn from movies and television that boys are in charge. They also are bombarded with commercials that encourage them to enhance their sex appeal with makeup, dieting, new clothes, and so on. It seems that half of today's films begin with violence against women, while they endlessly depict boys and men out for adventure.

From Jewish religion girls learn the same lessons of female subordination. We must change that impression, for it leads to the victimization of girls. Our religious communities in particular must be ever vigilant for signs of abuse and battery in the lives of people we know. I have encountered both men and women who have been traumatized by sexual abuse. The men I have known have suffered the same dislocating effects as the women.

Women and men who have suffered some form of sexual abuse or battery need our special attention. The trauma of abuse leads girls and women into drug addiction, prostitution, obesity, depression, and suicide. Assault and abuse induce an overwhelming sense of shame, self-hatred, self-silencing, and a belief that one is crazy and deserves the worst. Abuse destroys a child's sense of safety and trust. The crisis of faith in oneself and the world that results from abuse is one of the most serious issues religion needs to address.

To this end, Jewish communities can help foster healing by offering rituals that focus expressly on those who have suffered abuse. I present here two such ceremonies, one composed by a man, and the other by women. I encourage the use of the ceremonies for both genders. I honor the courage of both to face the wound and heal themselves.

The first ceremony was designed by several women in Nahalat Shalom who suffered incest at the hands of their fathers. All were in a support group or working with a therapist. This ritual was yet another way for them to work through their trauma and to transform their response to abuse from helplessness to action for the sake of their own lives. The ceremony satisfied several needs: the need to break silence and to tell the story, the need to grieve and to feel anger, the need to engage in physical movement to counter the experience of forced submission, the need to honor what they did to survive, the need to create a safe environment to carry out the ritual, the need to reinvest oneself with a sense of control, the need to break out of isolation and establish a new and renewed basis for friendships, the need to affirm the body and a sense of self-worth, and the need to have a Jewish context for the recovery process in addition to therapy taking place in the secular realm.

The ceremonial process is usually preceded by individual sessions with the rabbi of a congregation. People often take a long time to reveal experiences of abuse in such sessions. And I usually do not suggest the ceremony until much later. It is not the appropriate response for everyone. Let the individual lead the way. Every aspect of the ritual should feel comfortable to the individual and should not be imposed in any way.

Mikveh

Individuals may want to use the mikveh as a personal purification rite. At the mikveh, a short ceremony can begin with a blessing for all the parts of the woman's body.

Such a formula might be: "I bless my hair which is my own. I bless my eyes which are my own" and so forth.

As a woman dunks and comes up the second time she says the following:

       ❧   *A Thanksgiving for Renewal Through Immersion*

Brucha Yah Shekinah,
Ha'm'kadeshet oti u'm'hadeshet oti al yedei tevilah.
Blessed are You Shekinah,
Who consecrates and renews me
through the ritual act of immersion.

       ❧   *A Blessing for the Spirit of Life*

Brucha Yah Shekinah, who made me a woman.
Today I choose my healing;
today I choose a new covenant with myself;
today I choose to bless my body and my choices.
Blessed is the Spirit of Life who kept me
and sustained me and brought me to this day.

A Public Recovery Ceremony for Women

1. Set up an altar with the objects to be used in the ceremony. The people involved in the ceremony bring objects that represent their inner strength—for instance, a rock from a favorite beach, a letter from a good friend, a photograph of an important teacher.

2. The woman who has called the ceremony lights candles and reads a prayer she has written for the occasion. She may use the prayer that is offered at the mikveh.

3. The person who has called the ceremony invites everyone to join in a circle with her. Then they move to a simple dance and sing a song chosen by the initiate.

4. The group sits in a circle, and the woman tells the story of her abuse. A useful phrase for the telling of the story is, "I hold [*name*] accountable for [*specify the abuse*], which I leave behind me today." The recounting can be accompanied by the burning of strips of cloth that represent the torn fragments of the abused self. The community of

women at the ceremony can act as a beit din, a court of peers who affirm the reality of the person's experience.

5. The person next recounts a significant time in the first phase of her recovery process. For example, one woman shared this important dream:

"I was in despair and wanted to die. I was walking in the desert looking for ways to kill myself. I saw an old woman sitting on top of a mesa with a fire burning in front of her. I climbed the mesa and saw that she was a Pueblo woman, old and rather stern. Suddenly she shouted at me, 'Do you want to live or die?' I began crying and realized I wanted to live. 'I want to live,' I said back to her. At that moment I saw that there were really many women on the mesa sitting in a circle and singing. They were ancestor women, and they called me into the circle. 'I want to live,' I said. And at that moment I awoke."

The recounting of the story is followed by the phrase "I honor my courage in recovery." Recovery is a long, slow process that differs for each individual. We honor every step along the way.

6. The survivor then honors herself by naming positive attributes that helped her survive and by describing the progress that has been occurring in her life recently. This may be accompanied by anointing her with oil, the putting on of a special necklace, and/or the taking of a new Hebrew name. At the end of this part of the ceremony the woman wears any new ritual adornment that she has created or brought.

7. The community of women at the ritual honor their friend by holding a huppah over her head and guiding her to a specially decorated chair. Once she is seated, they present her with small tokens and gifts, which include poetry, stories, music, and food. Then food and drink are shared. Music can be used throughout the ceremony.

A Recovery Ceremony for Men

Several men have come to me over the years with stories of rape by strangers or abuse by mothers and fathers. Sharing their stories is extremely important for men, though society does not encourage them to do so. Rape crisis centers do not often serve men, especially since most male rape and abuse occurs in childhood or in the violent atmosphere of prisons. One Yom Kippur I was leading my community in a guided meditation before the "official" morning service. The meditation involved seeing oneself as the high priest, the cohen gadol, who was a medicine man, a shaman. He contacted death-bringing places in order to transform them into life-bringing spirits. He invoked the Presence of the Spirit of Life to turn away dangerous energies.

The congregation was guided to envision themselves in a place of natural beauty at twilight. They were to imagine being greeted by an animal guide and led toward the mountains. The animal guide showed them a hidden cave, which they entered. Inside the cave was a warm pool of water. They were to disrobe and stare at their reflection in the water and then enter the mikveh and imagine themselves as children surrounded by healing waters—healing the wounds of body and spirit. They felt the places that gave them pain and felt the water's heat opening and soothing those places.

I saw several people weeping.

We continued with breathing techniques. I directed the community to emerge from the mikveh and say a healing blessing. "By the side of the waters you see a new garment. The garment symbolizes your ability to face your pain and fear and heal yourselves through the medium of water and imagination."

We ended with a *niggun,* a wordless melody of a joyous nature. The community was then invited to share their inner journey if they so desired. Several people spoke, and after a while one of the men shared his vision. He had seen the man who raped him when he was six standing with him beside the mikveh. They both entered the water. The man disappeared and eventually emerged from the water as a smiling child. The perpetrator was gone, and our friend felt renewed. The congregation cried as he described his experience. Truly Yom Kippur, the holy day of at-one-ment and healing, of return to the home of one's soul, was accomplished for all of us through that experience. This man's sharing transformed the community's heart and soul that year, and it was also an important step in his journey toward healing.

A few years later, after the death of his father, he decided to create a
ceremony to adopt or take back his Yiddish name and to bury the past
that had harmed him. Several of us went into the mountains to be
present with him. He created an altar of objects and photos of his family. Part of the ceremony involved the donning of four prayer shawls.
One represented his link to his ancestors, since it came from an abandoned shul. One was his father's, one was his Bar Mitzvah tallit. He put
these three on one at a time, with a ritual act and a blessing for each.
Using a box he had made, he buried a tiny black dog made of wood,
which represented his childhood totem of protection. He then took on
his new name standing underneath the final tallit as if it were a huppah.
We honored his family as Levites and his craftsmanship as a wood-
worker and his intention to build an ark for our Torah. His partner
called me about two weeks after the ceremony and told me how joyful
"Simcha" had become. A shadow was lifted from his spirit, and he could
more fully embrace his life with joy. So may it be for all of us.

Epilogue:
The Journey Home

SPRING INTO SUMMER, each season with its memories. Solstice has always been a turbulent and visionary time for me, the season of Eshet Hayil, warrior of the flaming sword; she knows the way to Eden. One recent solstice I was basking in the hot afternoon sun and contemplating Shekinah, She Who Dwells Within, seeking an image that would encompass the whole of Her being. As I absorbed the heat, Dragonwoman, the primordial waterserpent, uncoiled in my mind's eye in all her terrible wonder. I saw her radiant beauty undulating beneath the surface of the earth. Her backbone formed the curved ridge of the Sandia Mountains, her mouth spewed forth the passion that burned in the furnace of her desire, her wise eyes melted the illusions of this world.

Shapeshifter and shaman, Dragonwoman inhabits the mist between realities, transversing dimensions to heal troubled souls. When she soars, her wings span the boundaries of the heavens; yet she dwells in the deepest recess of the watery abyss. Dragonwoman is the expression of women's unfettered power, divine Shekinah's essence.

In ancient times Dragonwoman was dismembered by societies that eviscerated women's political power and repressed the mythic images that once fueled our souls. In Jewish sources the female Leviathan was slain by God and preserved in brine as a dish for the righteous at the end of time. She was erased from the vessels of Jewish memory: stories and holy days no longer contained her narrative or her name. But Shekinah cannot die. She was, is, and will be. When she is welcomed in the light of day, Dragonwoman, like Lilith, haunts the shadows and whispers in our dreams: "Remember me."

At first I was uncomfortable depicting Shekinah as Dragonwoman. So, as always, I consulted with women friends. They all embraced the icon. Becky Narva thought that the fire pouring from the mouth of Shekinah represented the power of women's words. The circle of Rosh Hodesh women found Dragonwoman a suitable model of our physical strength and spiritual endurance, our wisdom and snaky sexuality, our fearlessness of mind. As the most ancient and worldwide icon of the Goddess, Dragonwoman can help us recover our lost sense of self.

Women's words and icons have been missing from Judaism. Denied the right to create the narratives that hold our people's memories and shape our values, women have existed as support staff for men. Our tradition taught us to look to men for answers. Today, as in former times, many seekers of Jewish spirituality are still drawn first and foremost to male rebbes and scholars for illumination of the Way. But this can only lead us into another room that is not our own. We need a fresh beginning. Shekinah is that beginning.

Where do we seek Her, She who has been hidden? We find Her in the negative images we are supposed to avoid, like Lilith the Demon Queen, in the deviant texts where God is not mentioned, like Esther and the Song of Songs. We recover Her presence in the neglected rituals and cast-off ceremonies of our lives. We come to know Her in the earth itself, in the body, and in the blood. From these places She reillumines our tradition. She gathers the broken threads of women's stories, songs, ceremonies, and customs and weaves a new garment for our souls.

Jewish women are finally emerging from the narrows of sexism, which for so long enslaved our hearts and minds. The Shekinah that calls us to Her place in the wilderness is not the god of Sinai (although She was there) or the passive feminine presence described in the kabbala (although She imprinted Herself in their words). She is the indwelling Presence that calls us to fullness of being. And the encounter is almost always unexpected.

Many summers ago I attended a woman's solstice camp in Harbin Springs, California. The heat was unremitting. Solstice afternoon, three hundred women shed their clothes, donned white plaster masks, and began dancing to the heavy thunder of thick-skinned drums. Sweat poured from our bodies as we gasped for air under our chalky masks. I felt dizzy as we swirled and stamped our feet on the parched ground. I went down in a heap. People thought I was having an ecstatic vision. Maybe so. I lost myself to hallucinations as the incessant pounding continued. I lay immobile for an hour under a large-rooted shade tree while Merlin Stone wet my neck and mouth with a damp cloth. After two days of vomiting and sleep I recovered. Solstice fever unhinged my rational mind. I was ready for magic.

This magic appeared in the unlikely person of a small, brown-eyed woman from Cuba with a gift for seeing what usually goes unnoticed. Flor Fernandez grew up in Castro's Cuba in a small village near a wood. At the age of twelve she was taken away from her family and subjected to forced labor in sugar cane fields. Eventually she and her family made their way to California, where she earned her Ph.D. in psychology and became the director of a family clinic in L.A. Her humble and generous manner and her sense of humor attracted me. We developed a lasting friendship. Soon I also discovered she had the ability to see spirits and auras.

One evening toward the end of camp, Flor and I left the evening program, hiked up a hill, and lay in the middle of a dirt road under the stars. As we gazed at the open heavens, I thought I would test her. For several minutes I visualized opening my third eye.

Flor glanced over and remarked, "Lynn, your third eye is wide open."

"Can you teach me to see auras?"

She said it didn't matter if I could see auras or not, as my healing powers lay in the way I told stories and made ritual. But she agreed in her easy and reassuring way to teach me what she knew. She told me to locate the white light around her body, which I did. She told me that even if I could not see auras, I could feel the energy field they generated.

"Try touching the edge of my aura, Lynn."

I reached over and felt the edge of the whiteness that surrounded her body. Suddenly I experienced a tremendous surge of energy leaping across me and entering my right shoulder. I bolted up, shaking.

"What's the matter?" Flor seemed surprised.

"I know this sounds strange, but I think a jaguar jumped over me."

"That was my animal spirit," explained Flor. "It's a jaguar. It must like you and was drawn to your energy. It wanted to make itself known to you."

Two days later the women of the solstice camp gathered for the final ritual under the midmorning sun. As I approached the circle, a green-and-gold snake slithered through the grass into the brush. Once again we shed our clothes, donned our decorated masks, and danced to the music of drums and our own voices. This time the sun's fire strengthened me. I felt in harmony with the earth, the sky, and my sisters dancing round. Shekinah's energy was rising. Here, far from rabbinic school, without the garments of civilization, I was naked under the sun, unashamed, hair blowing in the wind, my hands linked in prayer, surrounded by ululating voices. A rush of ecstasy cascaded through my bodyspirit, the roar of Dragonwoman resounded in my heart. I tasted her absolute freedom.

Slowly our energy became grounded as the ritual ended, and I drifted toward the outdoor showers to cool myself off. Two other women came over to say good-bye. We talked about our favorite people and events. Flor told me that two other women had also seen her jaguar. The three of us soon discovered our common experience and let the synchronicity sink in.

Shekinah is the synchronicity of spirit calling us home. She Who Dwells Within the heart of all being moves us to become fully human by breaking through the fears that paralyze our vision. She Who Dwells Within is the voice of women and men who demand an end to violence so that we can love one another. Let us celebrate Shekinah by cherishing the earth, honoring our creativity and uniqueness, and seeking justice in all human relations. Let us celebrate Shekinah by loving ourselves as Jewish men and women. I am a Jewish woman. Dragonwoman Shekinah roars inside me. Her Torah is the dancing Spirit of Life. Her Torah is within.

Notes

1. The quotations were culled from the *Newsletter of the International Committee for Women of the Kotel*, February 1991.

2. Suzannah Heschel in *Jewish Women in Therapy*, eds. Rachel Josefowitz Siegel and Ellen Cole (New York: Harrington Park, 1991), 33.

3. Susan A. Glen, *Daughters of the Shtetl* (Ithaca, NY: Cornell Univ. Press, 1990), 207.

4. Full versions of this tale with interpretation can be found in Sylvia Brinton Perera, *Descent to the Goddess: A Way of Initiation for Women*, and Diane Wolkstein and Samuel Kramer, *The Goddess Inanna*.

5. Geoffrey Hartman in *Midrash and Literature*, eds. Geoffrey Hartman and Sanford Budick (New Haven, CT: Yale Univ. Press, 1986), 16.

6. Tikva Frymer-Kensky, *In the Wake of the Goddess* (New York: Free Press, 1992), 17.

Index

240.0 GOT

She Who Dwells Within: A Feminist Vision of
Renewed Judaism

Gottlieb, Lynn